My Own Personal Apocalypse

Adriana C. Taylor

Table of Contents

1

I Was Just Lucky

The end of December is always an exciting time of new endings, new beginnings, new gifts, new faces, old faces. I used to not be afraid, not be scared of anything. Growing up in middle school, I never had any fears. I just wanted to be socially accepted by my peers. Until I started high school, the world became a whole lot bigger for me. I was so used to knowing everyone from elementary school. Now, there were strange teens I never met before. They became my new classmates. After several panic attacks, I was diagnosed with G.A.D. (Generalized Anxiety Disorder). I remember one day in my English class, my teacher asked the class what everyone's worst fear was. Some of my classmates said spiders. Others had said theirs was dark water. My teacher pointed directly at me and said, "What's your biggest fear?" I gulped. "My biggest fear... is the end of the world." My friend in the class gasped. My teacher then replied, "Our sun isn't even a dwarf star yet. We still have many years to come."

I'm not a very gentle person. Part of me loves hurting people, not emotionally, though I am honest about my feelings... I just love beating terrible men up... I was the firstborn tomboy in my family of four; not really much to expect, just a comfortably wealthy family living in the burbs in a livable forest. Ron, my current boyfriend, has to rely on his mother for the bread in his family, as his dad was or was not on probation. I can't quite remember, or he just doesn't want me to know. I was the bread and butter in my and his relationship. Just like his mother...

My phone lights up the room. I grab my phone while the message illuminates my blinding, cracked iPhone 8.

RON: I woke up at 1, but my phone was still not charged. What's up? How's your day been so far?

Me: Good. I woke up at 11, and I'm just chillin' watching movies in my PJs and eating popcorn with my family. You?

Ron: Very nice. Watcha Watchin'? I'm hiding from my uncle and little cousin, lol. They came over, and we talked for a little bit, but I really want to play my guitar today and just chill. We always do everything on Christmas Eve anyway, lol.

Me: Togo.

Ron: Who knitta? (He knows I like to knit scarves.)

Me: It's the new Disney movie about a Husky.

Ron: Oh, that sounds cute. I may look it up.

Ron: OH SHIT, MY KNITTA WILLEM DAFOE.

Me: Yeah, he's one of the dogs that brought the medicine for the children in Nome, Alaska, during the 1920s. Actually, all the credit should go to Togo instead of Balto. Balto just got to the town first. Togo actually traveled the farthest.

Ron: That sounds really good. I'm gonna have to check it out.

Me: IT IS.

Ron: How far are y'all into it?

Me: We just finished it. My mom loves it because it reminds her of my dog Skye. We just finished it.

Ron: Skye is the best girl.

Me: She is.

Ron: Skye is your mom's waifu.

Me: Pfft. Okay, nerd.

Ron: Just saying, Adri.

Me: lol, I Luv you. *I say that like I could. I don't think that I actually love him yet. He just decided to kiss me one day, and I just thought, hey, maybe I could fall in love with this man.*

Ron: I love you, too.

Me: Hehe, well, good luck with your guitar.

Ron: THANK YOU.

"Who was that, Adri?"

"Oh, it was just my boyfriend." *I can't believe I'm actually saying this, but he is my first real boyfriend.*

"Yeah, Ron is my boyfriend."

The whole room is just silent, like I just told them the news that the Easter bunny is real. The past few of my relationships were all a bust. Just a bunch of meme sharing peeps, and if I was playing chess with them, I was the pawn being played with because I was desperate for love, not just butterflies, but true love. Everyone has an ex-partner from their past they don't like to talk about. For me, all of their names ended up on the bottom of a police sketch pad. The butterflies I thought I had for them turned into wasps in my stomach. Sexual assault isn't justifiable by love. The home invasion shouldn't be cute and romantic. They should be in jail. Sometimes... I imagine myself straining and growing fangs from my mouth and claws on my hands to kill all of the men who thought they could use me. I freaking hate Twilight.

It's late; the Christmas lights are on, but they're on the lemon tree outside on a wire connected to the front of the house. I'm watching Star Wars in the living room of the house with a long entryway. I admire its humble beauty after it was remodeled and extended. It's the house my mother's family grew up in since 1988. My mother was born in Monterrey, Mexico, and my aunts, too. After my *tia* became obsessed with the Magnolia

Silos in Waco, they added on new rooms so that my *tia* Flora, and family of four, Marie, and my Abuelo, Carlo, could all live together.

As I write this, mi Familia is prepping tamales in the kitchen. My Tia, Anita, and my cousin, Maria, are preparing the masa for the Tamales. My mother is slaving away, cutting smelly Tripe. It's used to make menudo, but if you're around it when they prep it, it ruins the taste when you eat it. The memory of the smell of it when its raw just makes me want to skip it altogether. Yet I know if I don't eat it, my *tias* are going to be disappointed in me. The Tamales are saved for our traditional Mexican dinner: pork tamales, chicken tamales, cheese tamales, and even jalapeno with cheese tamales. Along with menudo, it's a soup with tripe, pork, or bacon, and hominy, along with other spices. It's not what I craved, though... It's the BBQ'd steak, chicken, and sausage accompanied by frijoles a la charra. I love my familia's cooking so much. It makes me proud to be a part of our family.

Luna interrupts my food daydream. She is a chihuahua. She's so small and frail, with a white crescent moon on her freakishly large forehead. She hops into my lap and curls up into a little ball before trembling on the blanket, covering my legs.

I want to stay up all night. I don't feel comfortable sleeping in a place I'm not familiar with, especially if that place is near the Mexican border. I don't know how my mother's family lived like this all these years.

Especially after living through a home invasion and a car theft – while my abuela was inside the car...

My abuela passed away in August of this year. She died of heart complications from swallowing her own tooth as she was being cared for in a hospice. It's no one's fault... I remember my aunts, uncles, and my mom staying with her through countless nights and days, sitting with her. Feeding her, bathing her. The oxygen machine, working day and night... She was in hospice for a year before passing away. One of her last wishes was to own two chihuahuas, just like when she first moved to America. My uncle Carlo bought two teacup chihuahuas, Sophia and Luna. Luna's eyes slowly started to tilt downwards as she grew up on Abuela's lap in her last days. Sophia remained unfazed and optimistic, yet Luna remembered.

I look at Luna's bobblehead with the permanent expression of sadness on her face. I stay up as long as I can in the renovated guest room while scrolling through the social media. Divulging in videos created by stranger of news about a virus spreading in China. I tried not to pay any attention to it. Instead, I see videos of chihuahuas and cats eating hot Cheetos as a high-pitched Hispanic voice plays over, saying, "I didn't ask to be born Latina, no mas Tuve suerte." Which means I was just lucky. Still chuckling, I induce myself to go to sleep at around three.

I wake up to the sound of crashing. My brain is still trying to register what is happening. I am not at home anymore. I am lying down on the couch in a busted-up trailer in a dusty, dried-up old crop field.

What's happening? Where am I!? I look for my phone to call someone; it's not on me. There's no one around, just the collapsing walls of an old trailer and giant gaping cracks next to the broken windows. I'm lying on a decaying, moldy couch. There's an old Panasonic TV above the wall opposite me. The cracks in the wall expose a dark, cloudy sky outside. It's a burning, blistering heat of a red sun with a yellow center. I look out at the crimson horizon of the trailer park. Cough and cough and cough. I physically can't stop coughing for 30 seconds. I can't even breathe; the air is so thick with smoke from an explosion. Gunshots from a rapid-fire gun go off outside. A stranger suddenly appears in the corridor to grab my shoulder. "Hurry up! We gotta get out of here," the strange voice beckons. They take my hand and grab their keys on the kitchen counter before leading me out of the front door to the right and into the outside street.

"Wait, who are you?"

"My name is Kaitlyn. I know a safe pla-" A telephone pole violently snaps above, sending sparks of electricity everywhere with wires thrashing about like giant live eels.

"Hurry, run!" Kaitlyn screams. She lets go of my hand and bolts to get behind the first thing she sees. I run with her. I don't look behind me. My legs move before I can even think about it, and I just run to an old 1995 black Chevrolet. She beats me to it. I catch up just in time. I see her crouching behind the front tire with her head ducked and her hands on the rubber tire. The top of the pole slams to the ground with a thud, narrowly missing the truck.

"Listen, I know where we can go. You just have to follow me." She says.

"How? I don't even know you." I reply.

"You just have to trust me, okay?" "The world is ending, but I know where it's safe..." she tells me.

"Where?" I ask. And then...

... I wake up...

2

The Last Christmas.

It's Christmas Eve, and I wake up to a hustling and bustling house. I check my phone, one unread message from Ron.

Ron: "OKAY, ASK ME A QUESTION."

Me: "OKAY. If you were famous, in what way would you be famous?"

Ron: "Oh, that one's easy. I'd want to be famous for my music."

Me: "Yeah, that sounds good. I would be famous for my poetry and art."

Ron: "You're an amazing artist; I could see you being famous in no time."

Me: "Thank you."

Ron: "You're welcome."

Me: "Your music has potential. Keep at it, man."

Me: "Alright, what does a perfect day look like to you?"

Ron: "Clear blue skies, 70-degree weather, sun shining. The usual."

Me: "Well, my perfect day is a trip to the beach. We have a picnic, I ride some waves, find seashells, and make a sandcastle. After the beach, we go to the local market to window shop. Then we go to a really nice restaurant overlooking the bay and have gourmet food and a piña colada."

Ron: "OH, THAT KINDA PERFECT DAY. I'm actually stupid."

Me: "Yeah, dude, like activities and such."

Ron: "Damn, I'm having a hard time thinking of a perfect day. Probably like going to the city during Christmas time, visiting Chinatown, getting something to eat, and then going to look at the lights. I am a basic white male."

Me: "Wowwww, you are."

Ron: "LoL, I wish it was my birthday, damn. Actually, not having a birthday on Christmas Eve would suck."

My mom stands in the hallway outside the guest room to put her coat on.

"What are you doing? Get up! We're going to eat at Cracker Barrel. If you don't get up now, we are going to leave without you!"

"Okay, okay, I'm up!" I say as I groggily shove myself off the queen bed against the wall. I can only crawl to the other side of the bed or jump off the foot of the bed. I choose the latter and step into my flats. Pull out a random, casual outfit, splash soapy water on my face, and run out the door before they close the front door.

We arrive at the Cracker Barrel with no worries. The waitress seats us down at a table for 8; I sit across from my sister Jackie. Anita sits on my left, and Marie sits across from Jackie. Valerie sits across Anita, and Via sits across Valerie. All of the sisters decide to sit across from each other, the oldest sisters to the youngest sisters. Unfortunately, I have the honor of being the first-born granddaughter of my maternal grandmother and the first child to attend college on my mother's side. I look at my messages; I still haven't replied to Ron.

Me: "Yeah, it would be harsh. You'd be a Capricorn."

Ron: "I'll stick with being the VIRGIN. Hey, when is your birthday?"

Me: "May 22nd."

Ron: "I feel like that is important info."

Me: "Yes, it is."

Ron: "Oh damn. Young ass bitch."

The waitress comes over to take our orders. I finally decide on a plate of French toast.

"Adri, can you pass the... that thing." Jackie points to the wooden peg game on my right side. I hand it to her.

"I love this game." Excitement brewing up in Jackie's face.

"Jackie, how do you even play that game?" Anita says. "I don't knowwwww," Jackie says with a smirk.

Typical... She's always been better at numbers than me. Algebra, Physics, you name it. I, however, love world history. So much so that I passed my AP world history class with a 98 and AP English with a 95. I shine where Jackie doesn't. She's dyslexic, unfortunately. We figured that out when I tried to teach her how to read when I was 8 and she was 4. We would both get frustrated as she pronounced her d's as b's and vice versa.

The smell of flapjacks floats around the table as the waitress plops a whole plate of pancakes in front of Via. "Oooooohhhh."

"You can't eat all of that." Valarie points at Via's daunting stack of pancakes as she swipes a lick of syrup with her fork.

"HEYYY! Mom! Valerie is eating my pancakes!"

We all laugh as the girls continue to bicker over a hot stack.

"Via! That's a lot of pancakes! Let Valarie have some."

"Okay... fine," she grumbles as Valarie takes a small triangle of pancakes.

She giggles and takes a bite. Not a moment later Valerie's plate is presented, there is a whole Belgian waffle. Jackie orders lunch. It is 11:35, and they're serving breakfast and lunch. Jackie ordered chicken dumplings and a side of apple dumplings. I cannot pass on French toast. No one else in my family likes French toast except for me. So I either have to make it myself or buy it if I want to enjoy it. After I finish stuffing my face, I pull out my phone to take a candid video of her as she picks off the little dumpling skins on her plate in a puddle of gravy. As she twists her face in disgust with her eyebrows and nose crunched. I turn my phone to the right, Maria looks at me blankly, and Anita chuckles. I posted the video on my phone. Ron lights up my phone with a message.

Ron: "Are those your cousins? LoL."

Me: "Yes, except for my sister, who's in front of me. U haven't seen her irl."

Ron: "She looks like your mom."

Me: "She does."

Ron: "What did she order??"

Me: "Chicken and dumplings."

Ron: "OOOO GOOD CHOICE."

Me: "LoL, yeah, hahaha."

Ron: "That's my favorite food of all time, my comfort food lol."

Me: "Oh? Bet with fried okra and corn."

Ron: "GODDAMN."

Me: "The good shit."

Ron: "Sounds like some good ass non-breakfast breakfast."

Me: "Yep."

Ron: "Or lunch now, I guess. Damn, I woke up late."

Me: "I thought this would be early for you anyway. Good morning."

Ron: "This is very early for me. I was expecting to wake up at like 3, but this is much better."

Me: "Yeeeee, I miss you."

Ron: "I miss you too. I was thinking about you a lot this morning."

Me: "Yeah, me too. Miss you."

Ron: "HEY, my phone is killing itself, but I will text you once it's charged a little. I'm sitting on 2%. I can't really use it and charge it at the same time. I know. This shit is ancient."

Me: "Okay, babe. Ttyl."

Ron: "Enjoy your French toast."

Me: "OKAY, I WILL."

After we leave the restaurant, my mom's family solely has one focus in mind: feeding our large family for Christmas Eve. I watch all my *tias* frenzy around the steaming giant pots of frijoles a la charra and tamales.

"Here." my mom hands me an apron.

"I need you to start making tamales. You need to start helping the family more." I get up from my spot on the leather couch. All she had to do was ask..."Muévelo perezosa..." She huffs under her breath.

"Okay, fine, I'll help." I relent.

I grab a corn husk in my hand and start to spread the masa over it. My aunt Patricia grabs one, too.

"Mira," she says as she takes a giant spoon and scoops a giant helping of masa. I do the same. She then plops the masa onto the corn husk in a dollop and then spreads the masa from the point of the husk to the center using the underside of the spoon. She smiles when she finishes.

"a ver." she gestures to me to do the same. I place the dollop on the husk and meekly spread the masa over the tamale. I repeat this 25 times and let my *tias* put in the pork meat of the Tamales. It's okay to be gay. I think, yeah, I'm not. But who knows... I could be.

"A si, a si, bueno." My Tia tells me. I let her wrap up the tamales cause, let's face it, I'm not housewife material that's kitchen-ready. I'm clumsy in the kitchen, and I really only know how to make pasta and Vietnamese spring rolls from my last job in the food industry.

I do what I can in the kitchen as my *tias* converse in Spanish. I can understand half of what they're saying. They laugh and carry on, kind, tender hands, constantly working over a pot of beans or a kitchen knife and cutting board, and it just feels good to be with them as they prep our Christmas feast.

It's not long before it turns four o'clock. My phone lights up; it's Ron.

Ron: "Henlo, I have returned."

Me: "Heyyyy."

Ron: "I'm getting ready for a Christmas party. Gotta go to a Christmas party at like 6."

Me: "Bet, hey, we never got to finish the questions."

Ron: "OH YEAH, how many did we do?"

Me: "4, I think."

Ron: "Yeah, I think so too. That's how many I counted. Okay, let me ask a question."

Me: "Ok."

Ron: "What's your secret skill?"

Me: "Hmmmm, singing."

Ron: "Is that really a secret, though?"

Me: "Hmmmm, kinda, or I can put sewing."

Ron: "Yeah, that works."

Me: "You?"

Ron: "I guess that could also be my secret skill? Idk this was a stupid question. Lol."

Me: "lol, no, it's not. Okay, my turn."

Ron: "Yes, go."

Me: "If you could live to the age of 100, would you rather retain your knowledge? Or keep your body young?"

Ron: "OOOO Okay wait, definitely keep my body young because then I could live to be older than 100."

Me: "Hmmmmm, it doesn't work like that."

Ron: "And I'll just start keeping notes so I won't forget shit."

Me: "You die at 100."

Ron: "AHHHH, retain my knowledge then."

Me: "Yeah, same. KNOWLEDGE."

Ron: "lol, alright, lemme think of a question."

Me: "Ok."

Ron: "If you could be any kind of fruit, which fruit would it be?"

Me: "HA!"

Ron: "Hard question."

Me: "A peach because they're sweet like me, and they got that ass."

I look up from my phone. Everyone seems to be ready and set to go. A huge stainless steel pot with a tinfoil lid covering is being carried out by my father.

"Careful, honey! You're starting to lean!" my mother cries out.

"It's fine," he replies, his face turning bright red from the exertion.

I run to the guest room and grab some mascara, swipe it on my eyelashes, dab a cream-colored nude eyeshadow, and finish off with eyeliner.

"Adriana, can you take the bowl of guacamole with you?"

I grab the Tupperware bowl of fresh guacamole on the white limestone countertop. We make the Christmas pueblo hop to my other *tia's* house.

In Mexican culture, from December 16th to Christmas Eve, children in Mexico often celebrate the "Posada" processions or Posadas. "Posada" is Spanish for lodging or Inn. Traditionally, they celebrate nine

Posadas, commemorating the Nativity when Joseph and Mary searched for somewhere to stay.

I remember when my Tia Marie's neighbors invited us to a Posada with a bounce house and a piñata filled with small toys and Mexican candy for all the children. It was a wondrous time.

The drive to the house makes me wonder what life would be like if my Mother's family never left Mexico for a better life. Huh, I would have never been born. The quiet town of Weslaco is made up of old pueblo buildings, separated by stretching palms and blooming *bugambilias*. We pass by the old bridal shop, Coco's attic, the antique shop, humble taquerias, and other shops that line the southern valley drive to the house.

Before we get to the driveway, a grassy, dry cow pasture greets us. We make the right turn to the neighborhood. A winding creek lines the backyards of the houses in my aunt's neighborhood. It's fiercely windy here this time of year. I step out of the parked car, ready and looking forward to this year's Christmas. Even if it is the first Christmas without my grandmother.

It's a lovely new home with tall ceilings, white marble tile, and white walls. My uncle had it custom-made for his family. I greet my family one by one. I haven't seen two of my uncles on the trip yet. Hugo and his family wave a friendly hello to me. Hugo's wife, my *tia* Aracelia, hugs me tightly.

"Hola, Adrianne, ¿cómo estás?"

"Bien, bien, Aracelia."

Suddenly, I'm greeted by a Chihuahua, followed by a ferret, and last but not least, a litter of kittens. I pet a kitten as it runs past my feet. I look around the home. The ivory tile supports my cheery, lovely family. All 15 of our faces are smiling and laughing from the reunion.

"Hahaha, Aracelia, aww, is that Frozen 2?" Jackie points to a new life-size vinyl poster of the new Disney Frozen movie.

"Yes, it's such a cute movie. The girls loved it. So now we can take pictures with it." She says that with a smile as she puts more bottles of Christmas liqueur on the marbled island counter, along with cranberry juice and coke.

The younger girls, Anita, Maria, Jackie, and the youngest siblings, go off to play in their room and gossip about the boys in school. Meanwhile, the Spanish-speaking adults are talking about how they are handling grandma's death in Spanish. I catch some words like "allá and aquí" as they complete the rest of the meal preparations. My dad talks to Hugo in his dad-to-dad voice mostly about each other's health and if he's going to go hunting with him.

Ron's notification lights up my phone.

Ron: "Okay, that's a good answer, lol. I would be a pineapple because I'm rough and prickly on the outside but sweet on the inside. Plus, they have sweet hair."

Me: "Awwww, that is a good answer. Okay, my turn."

Ron: "You go, Si."

Me: "Can you guess how you will die?"

Ron: "Easy, cancer. Next. I'm just kidding, lol."

Me: "Ooof, ummm yeah, I guess I am going to die of old age."

Ron: "Probably old age, but my next answer is going to be cancer."

Me: "Yeah, if you keep smoking."

Ron: "I stopped, biatch."

Me: "Biatchhh."

Ron: "It's been tough, but I managed to quit."

Me: "Nice, I'm proud of you. Anyways, it's your turn."

Ron: "Thank you, thank you. Alright, what would be the first thing you'd grab if your house was on fire?"

Me: "My bag, of course, which has my wallet and my phone."

Ron: "Understandable. I think mine would be my f***ing grandma because I know her ass would be asleep."

Me: "Oh nooooo."

Ron: "Lol."

It's not dinner yet, and I'm starting to feel my seasonal depression set in, and the thoughts of finishing up college in the spring are sitting at the back of my mind. Just waiting to get up and strangle me with code next semester.

"Ugh, I can't wait for college next year," I tell my Tia Aracelia.

"It's my last semester, and I have to finish my portfolio. And I don't have a lot of finished projects that I like."

"I'm sure you can finish it; plus, you're very talented, Adrienne."

"We still have Chloe's painting in Valerie's room."

"Oh yeah."

"She still keeps it up in her room." I painted an acrylic painting of their Bengal cat, Chloe, in a Marie Antoinette dress before Chloe was hit by a car, unfortunately.

"Would you like anything to drink?"

"Anything alcoholic?" she winks at me, then laughs.

"You are 21 now; you're welcome to drink in my house."

"Hmmm... can I have a... Vodka with cranberry juice?"

"Sure, miha." Aracelia then goes to a glass cabinet with liquor bottles behind it and grabs a Grey Goose bottle. She pours me a tall, skinny glass with ice. I take a sip...

"It's a really good one, one of the best drinks I've ever tasted."

"It's good, right? It's a Cape Cod."

"Just let me know if you want some more."

"Thank you, Ara-"

"Hey, what is this?" Hugo gestures to a plate of raw chicken.

"What?" Aracelia asks.

"At least put some pepper in it. I thought we were gonna marinate it in beer!"

"I put in salt. I thought that's what you wanted."

"Ay, Aracelia."

I escape to a room with old Hollywood charm to avoid their conflict. The ivory vanity is cold and comforting. I spot the source of all the kittens. A mama cat is lying down in a cage with a litter of grey and white kittens. I play with one of them with a silver chain. He paws at it and gets his toe beans stuck in the chain. He then tries to bite the chain "Pspspspsps..." I wiggle the chain to free him, but its paw is still stuck. I let go of the chain, and he just sits there. I try to pull the chain out, but it only drags the kitten on the white marble. I pick him up and manually free him from his chain. He mews at me in relief. I take a little video of him.

Ron: "OMG, I have to drive my mom b/c she's drunk."

Me: "Okay, lmaoooo, good luck."

Ron: "Thank you. I'll need it. Dude, I haven't seen my mom this drunk in a long time."

"Okay, everybody. Dinner's ready!" My mom yells as my uncle Hugo hands out a stainless steel bowl of charred chicken breasts, legs, and thighs. We all find a place in the house to sit at. All the adults who are 40 and over are sitting at the dining table while the 20 and under girls sit at the bar or the kitchen table. I'm next to Anita, who's eating the tamales my aunt passed out.

"Can you pass me the guacamole?" Anita asks meekly. I pass her the guacamole to the right. I indulge in a Styrofoam cup of a la charra beans. It's smoky and has a slight heat to it between bites of bacon and beans.

"Hey! Save some for me!" The girls, Via and Valerie, are fighting over chicken pieces. They both want a leg more than any other piece. Hugo comes just in time with a bowl of juicy grilled steak flanks in hand.

"Here, share some with Via." And puts a decent steak piece on their plates. The grilled goodness just kept coming through until my uncle finally came in with a bowl of pork sausage.

I'm halfway through a cheese tamale before I start to feel bad for Ron. My parents don't drink, especially my dad, not after living with a drunken father all his life. He didn't want to bring me up in the same household he grew up in. I'm grateful for that. I'm sure it's not that serious, though.

Me: "Wow, the tamales I'm having slap. Plus, my aunt made me a Cape Cod drink."

Ron: "Ooo, good, I'm big jealous. We just got back from my grandma's place. My mom didn't drink ANY water, just wine."

Me: "Ohh, Nooooooo."

While I am bemused at Ron's mom, everyone gathers in a circle around the living room. The Christmas tree is adorned with delicate lights and a red ribbon with a star at the top. The youngest starts opening their plaid-wrapped boxes. Via opens up her gifts, a neon rainbow journal and a Christmas letter she reads aloud. Valerie sits by the Frozen poster and opens a flat square package. She opens it. With eyes shocked, and mouth open in disbelief as she holds up a record of Micheal Jackson's 'Bad' album. We all exclaim, "Wowwwwww." The girls are excited, but I think her dad was more excited when she opened it.

"Hurry, put it on the machine." Hugo takes out the record player and removes the vinyl for Valerie and turns it on. I take a video of Michael Jackson's 'Smooth Criminal' bumping on a small baby blue record player.

Ron: "How's your party? Is it still going on?"

Me: "Look what my cousin got for Christmas."

I showed him the video of her record player with vinyl.

Ron: "Lucky... I know your cousin is so lucky."

Me: "lol, yeah, I know she's only 9, too."

Ron: "BRUH SHE GOT GOOD TASTE TF."

Me: "She gets it from her dad. Damn, all those records combined cost 200."

Ron: "UHHHH DAMN, she better listen to 'em. Those are nice records. The best song on that album, imo solid af, sounds great too."

Me: "haha, I love it when you get passionate 😊"

Ron: "I can't help it. I love Micheal Jackson, haha XD HEY, WHEN ARE YOU COMING BACK? Because I wanna drink with you. Just the two of us. That would be nice."

Me: "Ummmm, I come back on the 30th or 29th."

Ron: "Okie sounds good to me. Ah shI... wait, aren't we going to Carmen's dad's on New Year's? I forgot."

Me: "Depends. But we can drink before then."

Ron, "Okay, coI..."

Christmas Eve goes on. Everyone's laughing and being merry. I never realized, but My Uncle Juan strung up a piñata for us. The younger generations take turns hitting it until my sister hits it with the final blow. Candy splashes down on the girls as they scramble from the line onto the lawn, collecting as much Duvalin, Lucas, hot peanuts, and M&M's as they can. An orange that was stuck in the piñata falls and hits Via on her head. Everyone laughs. "Owww!" she exclaims. I let the girls have as much candy by not joining in. Instead, I steal a mango lollipop from my sister.

"Hey!"

"Come on, I didn't get any."

"Okay, but just one." she hisses.

I look at my presents. I received a set of journals with roses from my *tia* Flora, a necklace from my aunt Patricia, and $20 bucks from her husband, my uncle Carlo. I hop onto the pianoforte and play *Once Upon a December* after the record plays out. I even play the daunting *Requiem For A Dream* on the piano.

"Wow," says Via. "you play like an angel." Via and Valerie love it when I play piano for them.

Before I know it, Christmas Eve is over. It's 12 am, and everyone cleans out of the house as they carry out bowls of leftover beans, cheese tamales, and Christmas cookies. We all load up into the cars and head out with presents in hand. We drive back through the cornfields and small clay shops at night. It's comfortable in its familiarity to me. We stock the Christmas leftovers in the fridge, and I put my pajamas on and head to bed. I never expected Santa Claus to visit my home. Even when I was in the second grade, my parents confessed that Santa Claus wasn't real and that our presents were bought by them. It's 2 am, and I can't rest. I open up my phone and message Ron.

Me: "Merry Christmas, babe. Hey, what's up?"

Ron: "I'm on Discord with Austin. We're a lil drunk and listening to music. What about you?"

Me: "Chillin. Everyone else is asleep. I wish I was drunk with you."

Ron: "Hey, when you get back, we can. It'll be fun."

Me: "So Austin knows we are together?? What did he say? lol"

Ron: "He knows, and he's really happy for me and you, just said congratulations and stuff."

Me: "That's really sweet. Do you kiss and tell?"

Ron: "Noooooo. I told him after you asked me to be your boyfriend."

Me: "Oh, okay, cool."

I doubt that's all he said we had done. Tender make-out sessions for sure, yet when I went down on him for the first time, he seemed insecure about his size. Even though he's average size, as long as it works... He was my first boyfriend. At 21, I had no complaints. He treated me better than any guy I'd ever been with. He always gets my sense of humor, and I like him. Whenever I am with him, I am blissfully unaware of dying, like he's helping me get over my fear of relationships. He makes me glad I never killed myself that night...

3

The Beatdown

The boys were having a night to themselves. Ron went out with Eric, and they had just finished a rowdy game of pool at the nearest squalor of a pub. It's late, almost midnight, on December 14th, 2019.

"Hey, Eric, I really like this girl. You, you... Remember Adriana, right?" Ron says, stuttering as Eric drives him to his place in his Black MG 40 Roadster.

Eric: "Baby tycoon." His heritage is Italian and white. He was always sort of a legendary prankster at his school. He planned on becoming a movie producer, but the situation called him to be a landlord. "It must be so easy for him...." That's what everyone thinks about him. He's lost a lot of friends due to jealousy. Of Eric's three brothers, he is the youngest. Since a certain 'accidental' break-in at his mansion of a home, leaving his step-mother traumatized and put on medication, he's learned the ways of survival. And yet he has only one rule... No guns... His bunker is lined with all different types of knives, dull daggers, swords, katanas, nun-chucks, BB guns, tasers, taser guns, and baseball bats. He even thought about putting nails in a baseball bat just in case his zombie apocalypse dream came true. That night, he was stoned out of his mind. He thought he'd better stay away from a certain Californian hybrid. It's all about temperance, he thought to himself.

"I kinda feel bad, though..." Ron admits. "I am treating Adriana like the rebound..." They drive over a hump in the road. "After Carmen and I broke up our situation-ship," Ron remembers kissing Carmen's lips at Adriana's Halloween fortune teller get-together. He knows Adriana saw them kissing outside in the driveway through the window.

"Well, man," Eric raises his eyebrows with a smirk. "Aren't you the player now? —tch, I wish I was drowning in pussy like you."

"Hahahaha," they laugh simultaneously. Ron looks out at the flashing lights of the passing street lights along the darkened road. It's unlike him to be so careless with women. He feels like Carma is gonna get back at him for this. He pulls on the recliner lever on the passenger seat.

"Ugh god, it's like... These women can't get enough of my handsome... lovable... face." He caresses his face and his hair.

"Ugh, Duuuuuuude, get over yourself," Eric makes the next turn.

***

The next day, Ron asks Adriana to stay up late and chill at an old abandoned playground. Ron hasn't been working; he's been unemployed. He can't help this mentality. His grandmother always spoiled him growing up, and he felt like he was slowly growing into a hobbit—stuck in his room playing fighting games on PC.

It's like... she's such a strong woman. He likes that stick about her. She's ferocious—a force to be reckoned with. All their friends are gonna talk shit about her and him, saying classic lines like, "Hmmm... I wonder who wears the pants in their relationship." He winces at the thought. Buncha clowns! HA! Ron swings and plies on the swing. He looks at her; she's been staring at her feet while walking toward the playground. He knew it was coming...

"What's wrong, Adriana?" They stop at the darkened playground, only illuminated by one street lamp and the light of the moon.

"OH! It's nothing! I always look this way." Her face is a permanent frown when she's not saying anything.

"Why's that?" Ron swings in the dark, a lonely streetlight lighting up the abandoned park. He looks at the floor and the trees before looking to his right side at her. She's not swinging, just gently swaying back and forth, kicking up dust and sand.

"I don't know! I'm just stuck in a resting sad face." She giggles to herself. "I'm not ugly. I'm just sad." She starts to swing, but it's forced. There's a stranger in the distance...

"I used to hate swinging; it would make my tummy hurt as a kid if I swung too high." She confesses to Ron as she swings mildly. Her laughter slowly turns to tears the more she swings. He knew it was coming...

"What's wrong, Adriana?" She's crying as he sits on the swing.

"God, I love listening to Hozier." She grabs her phone and remembers her playlist. "I just don't know what I'm doing with my life anymore!"

"I thought I could do multimedia design... but... I'm failing—after effects."

"OH— I'm sorry that happened."

"What—?" She said, looking at him with wild tears in her eyes.

Her confession: ...It wasn't her fault... ...She's just a victim of a dare...

"Hey, I'm so sorry that happened to you, Adriana." Ron comforts her. "I wish I could go back in time and stop them from hurting you." His voice is soft and sincere.

"Yeah, sometimes it all just feels like a bad dream." She sniffles but looks more relaxed. "Ey, Yeah, College is a sideshow, that's why I never went.—Buncha

Clowns! HA!" Ron swings and flies on the swing. He winces at the thought. He looks at her; she's been staring at her feet while walking toward the playground. She laughs so hard that the swing shakes under her weight.

"Yep, it's been over four years now. I called the police and everything."

"You did!?"

"Yep!" She had this wild look in her eye and the smile of a deranged person. "I even stalked the man down and found out his birthday. To give to the police."

"Wow." He starts clapping for her and gives her a half-bow. She laughs, "OH, stop!"

Never mind. She's not a victim... She's a survivor... He thought to himself proudly, proud of her courage. He knew why he liked her so much. She was his girlfriend now, and he felt like he had to serve his duty to protect her.

***

And now... It was time for a stakeout, Ron thought to himself. Behind Ron's dreamy, happy-go-lucky attitude, he harbored a terrible anger. Knowing that somebody could destroy a beautiful girl's feeling of safety was enough to make him punch a hole in his bedroom wall.

Luckily, Adriana had confessed his name, that god-awful name. Ron remembered exactly who did it. In fact... He knew him from high school. So, to get the son of a bitch, Ron got a few of his buddies to stalk him and find out where he works.

The person of suspect: found.

The suspect vehicle: Black Dodge Ram 4-door.

The suspect license plate: ******.

All they had to do now was wait... Wait for that sucker to come out so the boys could take their revenge. For her...

"Hey," one of Eric's friends spoke out from the backseat.

"Why are we doing this? For all we know, she could be lying about it to get sympathy from you, Ron."

"Yeah, she's just a woman," another boy from the back jeered. The boys snickered in the back of Eric's roadster. The evil, ludicrous idiots.

"SHUT UP!" Ron snapped. "That 'WOMAN' is my girlfriend you're talking about."

"Life's not fair, dude... Why should we have to beat up some guy because he's a rapist? We could go to jail." — "He's not," the other boy in the back spoke up.

"You ASS WIPE!"

"He's the one who should be in jail. She called the police on him, but he's still walking the streets, a f***ing sexual predator!"

"Hey, hey, hey. Ron... It's okay," Eric talked Ron down from his seething rage. "I know exactly how to handle guys like this..."

***

Ron and Eric kissed the suspect's forehead.

...and beat his ass to a pulp...

Bloody and bruised, he sat with two loose teeth.

"How does it feel?" Ron spat—pth**—on his left eye.

"How does it feel... to be WHITE and ALRIGHT?" The boys sneered with revenge. Ron starts to feel like a real vigilante.

"I can feel it aright, you—yo... COCKSucker!" The suspect drunkenly sobbed.

Ron kicks his face into the pit. He rolls into a grass ditch with soot and gravel — covered in gasoline — from the Molotov cocktail they tried to force him to drink...

Ron punched, "—Ogh," him in the face where he spat on him ... leaving a glistening shiner on the bridge of his nose for free—

He lay there battered and bruised and burnt in the ditch—like he was already in an unmarked grave. He wasn't ready to die, though, he thought.

He crawled up bloodied and bruised... Like a boxer, after they lost the match, eventually, he found his phone and called his deranged mother to pick *cough* *burp* him up.

4

Friends till the end

I am at my friend Carmen's house, in her attic room. "Hey, let's watch 'Love is Blind,'" I suggest.

"Ahhhhhhh," I exclaim, clasping my hands over my face. I gasp, "I love that TV series!"

"Sameee."

Carma opens a bottle of white wine, and it tastes so good. "Do you like it?"

"Uh, I'm more into red wine."

"Are you sure about that?"

"Well, I did have a little bit of really good white wine when I was a flower girl at my aunt's wedding." We gather on her mattress on the floor and sit crisscross with a warm blanket over us.

We watch people talk and learn and feel through a wall. It was awesome; I could feel the love. An African-American woman and a white man fell in love, and...

WOW, mixed couples are so endearing. Love really is blind.

Oh, how beautiful life is.

To see a love I never had.

***

I leave the next day for my aunt's house.

We spent the rest of our stay in Weslaco playing Monopoly with my family for hours, only for me to lose to my *tía* Flora's double hotels.

Reports were being made on this new disease emerging from Wuhan, China, affecting the respiratory system and weakening the victim. After watching TV on the couches, my mom made us all clam chowder with wine. It was a good break from the tedium and drudgery of the constant news reports on fires, tornados, floods…. I can feel it. The end times are here.

***

We've made it back from the six-hour journey; it's the 30th, and I'm getting ready for Christmas with my friends.

Ron: "Lemme know when you're ready."

He texts me, but we still have plenty of time before the shenanigans commence. It's only 8, and I'm putting eye shadow on.

39

"So what's going on?" My mom's voice carries up from downstairs.

"I'm just getting ready for Christmas at Carmen's house," I say as I slightly open my mouth to put on my eyeliner.

"Oh, okay. Well, don't wake us up if you come home at 4 am in the morning," she yells from downstairs. "Last time, you woke us all up with the dogs barking." I can hear the twinkling of my dog's collar as he shakes.

"I'm sorry—"

"Text me if you're sleeping over or coming home late so I can leave the door unlocked."

"Okay, Mom, I'll let you know."

She's always worried about me staying out late, even though she knows I'm with Carmen. We've been friends since sixth grade; I still can't believe we've stayed friends this long. I put on my peach sweater. Mom says it looks nice on my skin. I spray on my Calvin Klein Eternity perfume while putting on earrings to complete the look. It's a nice 68 degrees outside; I don't have to worry too much about layering up before heading out. There's no snow. The grass is dry yellow, and the trees are bare or full of umber and orange leaves.

Carmen works at the Homewood Suites hotel, so she gets off work at 11 pm. We agreed to have a Christmas party to exchange Christmas presents. It's not unlike us to hang out this late because of her work hours. We usually come together at 8 or 11, sometimes later. We'll end up sleeping over at her house or staying up late enough to meet her mom, leaving for work in the morning.

I drive over to Ron's to pick him up. It's a straightforward drive from my neighborhood to his. I pick him up in my white Hyundai; I pull up to the sheltered parking spot, and he walks out in his signature plaid shirt, unbuttoned with a band t-shirt underneath and baggy denim jeans. He opens the passenger door.

"Hey, Ron."

"Hey, babe."

"How was your trip?" He says just before meeting my lips for a kiss.

"It was good; presents were obtained, memories were created," I say like a robot, but I smile at the end like it was all a joke.

"Oh yeah, Ha ha."

"I was texting you this whole time!" I smile with my vampire, rabbit-toothed grin and shove his shoulder.

"Just checking. I got your present." He looks down at his backpack. "Me too. I have everyone's present," I motion to the stack of wrapped boxes in the back seat.

"Oh shit, hold up. I forgot Carmen's present. Be right back." He yells after he sets the backpack down. His apartments are to the right of an elementary school and in front of the baseball fields. The fields are in front of Lake Houston, it's a small park, River Grove Park. It's the lake I used to visit growing up. I roll down the window; I breathe in the humid air and remember the winding lake with tiny islands that used to look big when I was little. I remember stomping around their pebbled beaches, looking for treasures, or even hoping to see a mermaid in the emerald-green waters. I did one day manage to find a rusty machete in the forest behind the soccer fields of River Grove Park when I was tall enough to ride the roller coaster.

"Hey, I found it." He interrupts my nostalgia, holding an unwrapped box.

"Alright, let's go pick up Trent."

I turn on the car, slowly back out of the parking lot, and head down the road. Trenton's house is all the way on the other side of the subdivision. Just before the ritzy mansion neighborhood in front of a man-made lake, I pass the small shops to make the trip.

"Hey, text Trent, we're here," I tell Ron as I pass by Sonic's drive-thru.

"I'm on it."

I take a left turn to dip into his part of the world. His home is a comfortable two-story home with red brick and a white garage door.

"Hey!" I honk my horn with a small tap. I look around the darkened neighborhood.

"Shhhhhh! His family is asleep." Ron scolds me.

"Oops, I forgot it's almost 11:10." A light inside the window above the garage goes off. Trenton strolls out of his house. His skinny body is swallowed in a black long-sleeve shirt, khaki pants, and bright neon Nikes. His hand carries an athletic bag full of presents.

He clears his nose, "...Ah, what up, losers?" he sneers as he opens the back seat door.

"What up, dude, how's your balls?" I grab my stomach and start absolutely laughing my ass off at Ron's quip.

In the Bible, it says, well basically, that if a man's balls are hurting, he's hurting his future baby mother's heart.

"Shut up," Trent says, but he's grinning too.

"Merry Christmas, Trenton. How was your Christmas?"

"Uh, fine," he groans as he slides into my back seat. He immediately grabs the cord for my aux to start playing Smashing Pumpkins - Mayonnaise. I make the mundane drive through the temperate forests to the sound of a wailing electric guitar. It's Ron's favorite song. The traffic lights are almost like fireflies guiding us home in the dark. I roll my windows down to feel the cool winter breeze. It's not cold enough to snow, but it is cold enough to see your breath in the air. The way to Carmen's is toward the front of our subdivision. It's also the lowest point of Kingwood. I drive downhill through her neighborhood. Drainage ditches are dug alongside the road. The houses open up to a clearing, a field of tall grasses and flowers with a creek on each side of the field appearing on each side of the road before disappearing behind more cottage-like homes. When we finally arrive, I park in the road to avoid being yelled at by her mom. Her house is a one-story brown brick house with a large attic. It has to be; that's where Carmen's room is. I text her we're here.

Carmen: "Come on up."

The guys and I grab our stuff before walking up the driveway. Tall pine trees grow lengths in her front yard. The driveway branches out to a parking spot separate from her garage. We pass the front door and make our way to the right side of the house to the backyard gate. Carmen is there to open the gate. She stops and looks at us with all our boxes in bags.

"Awww, really? You shouldn't have," Carmen says, smiling sarcastically at Trent.

"You're right, I shouldn't have." Trent retorts. I laugh. "Hey, Carmen."

I hug her despite my hands being full. We enter her backyard, and suddenly, I'm greeted by a huge curly mop of a dog. He jumps and claws up my leg.

"Cooper! Cooper, no! Down!" His ivory mopey hair flying up and down, he jumps off and runs to attack Ron instead.

"Silly boy," I say as I look at Ron. "Hey, buddy." He says before giving Cooper a quick pat on his head. Cooper takes it as an invitation to jump on him.

We make our way up the rickety brown stairs to her room on the second story. The wooden stairs are so worn out that the fourth step is loose from one screw. Once we get to the top, we reach a platform that reminds me of a crow's nest. If you tried to climb up the railing, you could reach the roof of the house.

That's where Ron Smith and I sat in September when we first started hanging out and had intimate discussions past midnight. Ron actually had a crush on both Carmen and me at the same time in October. He even made out with her when they were drunk at my Halloween party. That was before she turned him down when he asked her to be his girlfriend. It almost ruined the group's friendship. That's why we had to keep our relationship a secret from Carmen and Trent. I didn't really care if Trent knew, but if he knew, I know he would confess to Carmen that we were together. Secrets don't last long between us. I did not want her to get mad at Ron for moving on so quickly and being reckless with our feelings. I have nothing against Carmen; I just don't want it to ruin our friendship.

Carmen starts to unlock her bedroom door. She's wearing a mauve shirt and a grey-knit sweater over it.

Her sweater hugs her large bust. Carmen opens the plaster door. Her room is long and narrow. The ceiling is 8 feet high and slants to 5 feet on the right side, making a 45-degree angle. The walls are shaded white, and the floors are cream-colored wool carpets. Near the front door is a white vanity with her makeup scattered over the glass top. There's a white dresser on the other side of the room. A round glass coffee table takes up the space between the dresser and the white vanity. Her bed is near the back by the restroom. Her whole room is connected to a bathroom with no doors to separate her room from the bathroom. Next to the vanity, a medium-sized TV sits on top of a bookshelf made of white squares with books and pink folders inside. Beside the bookshelf is a mini fridge with a microwave on top. It's nestled on the border wall separating the room and the bathroom toilet. A light pink faux-fur rug invites us to sit in front of the TV.

"Sorry about the mess," Carmen refers to her room with her hand.

"It's cool; mine's worse," Ron comforts her.

"Take off your shoes before you come in. You can sit wherever you want; there are Trulys in the fridge and a bottle of vodka."

I look at the fridge in the back. "Sweet, thanks."

"That's haram," Trent groans, but I know he's about to dive into the fridge soon.

I place Trenton's presents on the glass table and the other on the floor. Trent bends his slender legs and places his presents on the floor by Carmen's golden mini-Christmas tree. I could almost make out what his presents were inside the grocery bags. Ron sets his brown paper bags down by the bookshelf. As soon as everyone is settled in, Trent walks towards the back and launches himself onto Carmen's bed.

"Ugh, I'm going to take a nap," Trent groans, voice muffled in the sheets.

"Noooo, stay up with us."

Under the pillow, his cheeks are flushed; he always acts stoic and indifferent, but I could tell he was embarrassed to give everyone Christmas gifts this year.

"The first one to fall asleep gets their hand in hot water," Ron threatens him, standing hunched over from the low-angled ceiling.

"Yeah, how big do you want that penis drawn on your face?" I smirk at him.

Trent grabs a pillow and slaps me in the face with a *whomp*. "Hey!" I retaliate with another pillow. *Foom* he blocks it with his hand. While he's distracted by me, Ron grabs one and hits him in the back of the head with a thud.

"Really, dude?" Trent realizes he's being double-teamed and grabs another pillow for Ron and whams him good. They hit each other over and over like they were in high school again. I start to laugh at them.

"Hey! Hey, stop it! You're gonna break something," Carmen warns them. They stop; Ron drops his pillow on my head.

"So..." I look around at everyone. "What are we gonna do?"

Trent falls back on the bed before slamming a pillow in his face. "I am... going to open this Truly," Ron declares while opening up a frosty passion fruit Truly from the undeniable mini fridge. Beckoning me to grab one, before he closes it, I come in to answer the call. I grab a lime Truly with the promise of becoming buzzed and blissfully unaware that I have work in the morning and the fact that there's a growing pandemic in China.

"Oooooh, let's play a drinking game," Carmen pulls out the stack of dubious drinking games from under the glass coffee table.

"Hehehe, what about my truth, dare, or shot game?" I ask. We've had many a night where we would get shit-faced to this game. In the game, there is a spinner that lands on truth, dare, or shot. If it were to land on shot, it was either one to three shots. If it landed on truth or dare, you would have to pick up a card from a deck of truths or dares. One of the truths is to confess if you have a crush on one of the players. One dare dares you to swap a piece of clothing with the player to the left. *Underwear included* I swapped my shirt to Carmen's friend Manuel the last time we played. I can still see my cute white crop top sheathed over his buff chest, barely covering his nipples. "Uh oh, nip slip!" Carmen remarked while stupidly drunk as she tried to cover his exposed nipples with her hands. I look around the room.

"We... will... not... be playing that game tonight," Carmen looks at me with wide eyes.

"Yeah, I still have flashbacks," Ron pretends to shiver.

"Okay, what about the buzzed drinking game?" Carmen pulls out a black deck of cards. Without warning, Trent grabs a hold of the box from her hands, shoves them underneath him, and sits crisscross over the cards.

"What the hell, Trent!?" Carmen exclaims while punching him in the arm.

"What? I am tired of playing this game. We already asked all the questions." We all stare at him.

"I know all your tattoos, Carmen. And I know everyone's porn preference. And—" I double over laughing on the carpet. She cuts him off before he can reveal any more embarrassing facts he remembers. "Okay, fine... What would you rather do?" Carmen asks Trent, who slowly gives the cards back to her.

"I want to open my presents," Trenton says like a spoiled child.

"Ughhhhh, fine, we'll open presents first," Carmen groans as she rises from her spot on the floor. She steps over us, makes her way to the bathroom, and returns with decorated gift bags. Carmen hands one to me. "Thank you, Carma!" I say, using her nickname, and look around at everyone exchanging gifts.

I look at Ron as he hands me a plain rolled-up brown paper grocery bag. "When I was growing up, I never believed in Santa Claus," I confess. "Wait, seriously?" Ron looks at me in disbelief, appearing a little sheepish.

Carmen's shocked face softens. "Really?" she asks. "My dad used to dress up as Santa when we were little, and he would show up on Christmas morning and give us stockings with toys. Until his beard came off one time, and we all figured out it was my dad the whole time." Carmen smiles softly, remembering her past.

I look back to Ron in front of me. "Yeah, that's kinda what my parents did, but we would go and take pictures with Santa at the mall. I used to think that was the real Santa," Ron confesses before taking a swig of his drink.

"Christmas is just another holiday created by capitalism to get us to spend more every year for the supposed birth of Jesus Christ," Trent remarks. "When we all know he would've been born in April if he did exist. We shouldn't even be here."

I glare at him. "Shut up, atheist!"

"Yeah, Trent, then why are you here exchanging gifts with us?" Ron spits at Trent. "Go home and burn a bible or something." We all crack up with laughter at

Ron's retort. Trent huffs his grape-flavored vape at the comment.

"Okay, who wants to start opening gifts?" Trent takes Carmen's gift and starts to unravel it.

"Wait... let me grab Haru."

Haru is Carmen's new pet guinea pig. Carmen has a thing for spontaneously buying small rodents and losing them. Like the time she brought a rat home, and it died from the cold weather after her sister forgot to turn up the AC after Carmen went on a trip. Carmen brings her orange and white guinea pig into the group and holds Haru like the Godfather held his cat in the clutch of her left arm. She lowers herself to sit criss-cross to the right of me, between me and Ron. Carmen scratches his nose before Haru burrows into her arm just in time for Trent to open his gift. He opens up the Christmas gift bag to a deep-space-blue Star Wars tin lunch box.

"Awe — no way, dude," he says, and as he says "dude," his Adam's apple flexes in his throat. "Do you like it?" Carmen says, watching him enthusiastically.

"Yeah." He pulls out a pair of matching Star Wars socks from the bag. "And this pair of socks. I needed some, actually." Trent smiles wide and grabs the tin lunch box. "Let me open this bad boy up." He takes out his pocket knife, seemingly out of thin air, and starts to cut open the clear plastic clinging to the lunch box. "This man brought his KNIFE!" Carmen remarks incredulously.

"I did too," Ron speaks, looking up from trying to figure out what I wrapped in his gift. "I need to carry my kni— Always come strapped," Trent interjects.

Trent turns around and pulls out a small box from his grocery bag of gifts. "Alright, bro, ahhhh, here's your gift."

"Dude, sweet, you didn't have to." Ron receives the black box for a vape. It's unwrapped and clearly visible. "I actually needed a new one. The coils in my last one stopped working."

"I hate when that happens," Trent nods to Ron. "Thanks, bro." Ron gets up and leans into Trent on his right fist, bumps him, and pats him on the back.

"Are we gonna open presents in order?"

"...So I guess I'll go next."

"Here." Trent hands Carmen a bag. She pulls out a flat square from the bag. It's a vinyl of the band Tool. Carmen looks embarrassed by his gift.

"Oh, um... Thank you, Trent."

"What's wrong?"

"Do you like it?"

"It's great. Thank you. It's jus —um. I already have one."

"Oh..."

The atmosphere of the attic room becomes stale with disappointment. She looks taken aback. "It's okay... I can return it and buy you something else," Trent offers.

"No, no, no, it's fine, really. I'll just keep a second one if my first one breaks, or vice versa." Meanwhile, Ron opens up his new chrome vape and reads the instructions. He toys around with the vape like a man first discovering fire.

"Here, Merry Christmas..." Trent finally gets to me. I was surprised the day before Christmas, he texted me:

Trent: I haven't bought anything yet. But Ron, I want to get him a vape. I'll think I'll get Carmen a plant? But I'm not sure.

Me: Hmmmm, okay.

Trent: And you like art supplies and plants.

Me: Succulents... Yes.

Trent: RIGHT, SUCCulents.

"Oh, nice, thanks, Trent." I roll my eyes at his comment. Men can be so pitiful at times.

In my hands, I held a bulbous planter with a spike leaf cactus growing atop it. Even if it's not a succulent plant, it's a nice gesture, especially coming from Trent. Ron turns around from his spot on the floor to grab his bag of gifts.

"Alright, everyone, close your eyes." I look around as Carmen and Trent close theirs before I do. "Okay, hold out your hands."

"Seriously, Ron, Nooooooo, it better not be anything weird," she said. "It better not be something gross." I hear Carmen's voice groan. We laugh. Something hard and bumpy drops into my palm. "What is this?" "Okay... Open." I open my eyes and look down to see it's a pack of chocolates shaped like liquor bottles wrapped in foil with Jim Beam and Bacardi labels.

"They're alcoholic chocolates. Sorry, I couldn't afford something else," Ron apologizes. "It's okay," Carmen consoles him, looking at the gold and silver aluminum foil-wrapped chocolates.

"Thanks, man, I love these."

"Yeah, thanks, Ron. Now we can really get drunk."

"Thanks, Ron, we appreciate it." Carmen unwraps a bottle.

"I literally just stole these from my parents' liquor cabinet." He confesses. I open a Jim Beam chocolate. I unwrap the copper-colored foil to reveal a milk chocolate coating. I take a bite from the top. It's golden, boozy, sweet syrup adjoins my tongue with a kick of alcohol.

"Mmmm... The Jim beam is good."

"I wonder if this is equal to the amount of alcohol in a shot."

"It's probably a little less than half a shot," Carmen answers me with chocolate in her mouth.

From the corner of my eye, I can see Trent grab my gift by the peace lily plant.

"Oh, here it's from me, Merry Christmas Tr—" he's already cut the ribbon.

He unwraps the white and red bicycle wrapping paper from the first package. I gave him two presents, wrapped separately but tied together with the same ribbon. He tears the corner of the bag. As soon as he sees the red and pink of the plastic, he immediately rips off the rest of the paper and ravages the bag to get a piece of Twizzlers (his favorite candy).

"Ooo, can I just..." He gives Carmen a piece and begins to tear open the second box. I had no idea what to get him. Trent isn't into sports or hunting. He just sits around playing video games, drinking Mountain Dew, and reading Wikipedia pages for fun (I'm not joking.)

"Oh, hahaha." He laughs in a strained, high pitch. Carmen smiles at his laugh.

"What?"

"Look."

"Caption This: Fail Army."

"Oh my god. Adriana, what did you buy this man?"
She asks me.

"Hey, it could be fun. We should play it tonight
after we open all the presents."

"Wait, dude, let me see." Trent hands Ron the box.
Ron looks over the arrangement of ridiculous and
stupid pictures on the front and chuckles. "Okay, but
we have to play this game tonight."

"But first, here." I give him a red, flat, and square
package with a smaller box on top tied together with
gold tinsel.

"Merry Christmas, Ron." I almost call him babe.
He opens the smaller package first.

"Oh man, nice! I could really use this." I found
Ron one of the last survival kits in the men's section at
TJ Maxx. The inscription reads survival kit. Adventure
Awaits. Includes 7 tools, an essential camping
companion.

"It's got a wire saw, tweezers, rope safety pins, flint
and steel, and a Swiss army knife. It's perfect if we
decide to go camping," I assure him.

Trenton gestures to the flat square package. "It's
obvious to me there is another gift in there."

"Yeah, hopefully, it's not another record for Tool."
Ron chuckles at my retort.

"Hey, I wouldn't mind, though. But I don't have a record player to play it on." He converses with us as he slowly rips open the gift wrap.

"No way!" It's a Dragon Ball 2020 calendar. "Thank you, Adri." Ron smothers me in one of his bear hugs.

"Wait, lemme find my birth month."

We finally finished with my gift to Carmen; a glass Hello Kitty cup and a four-pack of frosted Hello Kitty shot glasses. "Awwwww, thank you, Adri!" Carmen hugs me tight. "Wait," she smiles. "I know the perfect drink to serve in this." She gets up and grabs a liquor bottle from atop her black mini-fridge in the corner. Puts ice in her new cup. She turns around and shows us the liquor. It's a tall rectangle-shaped bottle with a red square cap called Hammer and Sickle, Imported Russian Vodka (the good stuff). Carmen holds up the Hello Kitty glass and the Russian vodka together.

"Oh, you know..." Ron lets out a burst of laughter. "Communist kitty."

"Based..." Trent lifts up his glass. "To our comrade, Hello, kitty." He croons in a Russian accent. Carmen takes a long swig of vodka from her glass before handing me her gift.

"Thank you, Carma." We hug, and I tear into the gift bag. Inside is a pack of Burt's Bees lip gloss and a book about Astrology. My sign is Gemini. Trent is

Virgo, and Ron is also Virgo, but I don't hold it against them. And Carmen is Sagittarius.

After all the presents were opened and all the vodka was gone, we spent the next hour playing Trent's card game. The object of the game is to have a judge pull out a funny picture or meme. The three other players have to pull seven caption cards and find one that matches the picture and give it to the judge or vice versa. The players find a picture that matches the caption. We got up to stretch our legs and sat on the carpet in different corners of the room to play the game. I sat where Trent was, and Trent sat where I was next to Ron. Carmen sat next to me behind the glass coffee table, which made her reach for her cards.

"Okay, okay, this is for the caption; when they don't reach for their wallet on the first date." Carmen holds the three cards and pulls out a picture of a raccoon reaching over to grab a stack of cash. Giggling ensues as we sit together in a broken circle on the floor around her glass coffee table. The next card she pulls out is a Chihuahua with false eyelashes looking dead-eyed at the camera. More giggling continues.

"Real animals being tested on, oh… the humor." She pulls out a baby with a frowning face in a high chair.

"Okay, the Chihuahua wins."

"Yes! thank youu, thank youu." Ron grabs the caption card as a reward.

We play the game until 2 AM, until we decided the game got too stupid to keep playing.

5

My lips + his lips, apocalypse.

"Hey, let's go outside," Carmen says, getting up and stretching her arms.

"Yeah, it's getting stuffy in here," I reply. We're still lightheaded from laughing our asses off at the card game. We all get up from the indents we made on the ivory carpet and go outside. The lights from the stars and the porch light make Ron's skin glow as we all stand on the square foot balcony.

Funny, I didn't exactly fall in love with Ron Smith. I was the one to pick up the pieces after Carmen said she couldn't return his feelings. Carmen was a dead end, and I was the green light at an intersection. I was the clearing of the back roads for him, his Escape. Letting his vehicle drive right through my heart.

I look at the boys again as they light up their vape smoke.

"Wanna hit?" Ron asks me, handing me his vape.

"Sure," I reply, taking a huff from his shiny new vape. I cough a little as it comes through my nose; its pineapple essence burns the back of my throat, yet it tastes refreshing in my mouth.

"I think I am going inside," Carmen announces, opening the white, plaster door and entering her attic room, leaving just Trent, Ron, and me to ourselves.

"Want to hear something strange?" Ron asks us. "One night I was playing Street Fighters in my room, and I heard one of the neighborhood cats screaming. I look outside, and a teen couple had broken into the apartment pool and jumped in with a cat."

"Poor cat," Trent comments. He does have a soft spot for animals.

"Did they get caught?" I ask.

"No, they got away with it."

"Dude, what are your stats on the PC?"

"For what?"

"For the new Street Fighter game."

The boys start talking about video games, and I tune them out. I begin to think about the past year and how it's almost over. 2019 is almost over. I smirk to myself as I think about the running joke that we will all finally have 2020 vision next year. I am excited for next year, really. It's a new and intriguing feeling to say I have a boyfriend now.

I have been ghosted by boys so often my phone should be haunted by now. But here he is sitting on the railing, smoking his vape. Ron's not too handsome, but he's not ugly either. He's kinda chubby, and his face is covered by his aviator glasses, framed by straight long ash-brown hair. He looks like a younger version of Jeff Bridges; the Dude in the Big Lebowski.

He leans in as he steps off the railing. Their conversation stops.

"I'mma go inside," Trent tells Ron.

"Alright, bro."

I look off into the distance. The next-door neighbors are smoking and drinking beer on their porch.

"Hey, you okay?" Ron asks me.

"Yeah, I'm fine, just people watching the neighbors."

"Oh yeah? What are they doing?" he asks me.

"Just standing around drinking beer. Wait a minute, isn't he a cop?"

"Ex-cop, he's an ex-cop."

I look over at the man. Good thing we aren't smoking weed.

"Oh... hey, can I get another hit from your vape?" he looks down at me.

"Sure... but you have to kiss me first."

I smile at him, "oh?"

He drags his vape. "Come here."

I do, and with a light touch, he brings my face to his. Our lips are an inch apart as he gently blows vapor into my mouth. His hands clasp the small of my back. The moon knows our secret, passionate affair. I inhale his smoke like he's my drug before we collapse into a slow heavy kiss.

"What are you guys doing?"

We turn around abruptly; it's Carmen at the entrance.

Oh shit... My heart drops. She wasn't supposed to find out like this.

"You guys are..." Her eyes widen with amusement.

"Together?"

"Yeah," Ron answers her.

"W- we kept it a secret cause we thought you would be upset," I try to defend ourselves.

"No. I am mad because the fact that you HAD to keep it a secret, like you guys were doing something wrong. Especially after you went after me, Ron," Carmen yells at us fervently. She glares at Ron with fierce anger.

"You just had to date someone in the group."

"It's not like I can control how I feel, Carmen," he steps closer to confront her.

"Oh yeah? By having feelings for both of us?" Carmen challenges him by stomping her foot on the crows nest; the umber wood board creaks. Ron looks down, ashamed but he doesn't say a word because he knows it's true.

I wince at those words. I do not want to be here. I wish I could just float up into the night sky and let the angels take me.

"Whatever, just don't let your feelings for both me and Adrienne get between our friendship."

"I won't."

Carmen gestures to me. "Come with me. Now!"

I follow her into the room. The wood boards under my feet start to creak, I can see the rocks at the bottom through the cracks. I've lost almost all hope of us being friends. We've been friends since middle school; I don't want to lose our friendship just because of my relationship with Ron.

I step into the room after her.

"Hey Trent, get out," Carmen kicks Trent out of her room.

"Are you serious right now?" he says before dragging his vape, as he's 6 feet away on his phone sitting on Carmen's bed.

"Yep."

He huffs a cloud of smoke, "Tssss... whatever."

Trent gets up and slinks out of the room. The door shuts behind him.

Carmen turns to face me with eyebrows furrowed. "There really was no reason to keep it a secret."

"You know you could have told me." She stomps around the room.

"I know, but after you friendzoned him that night, I thought you'd be mad at me for going out with him."

Carmen finally decides to sit down on her bed facing me. "That's not true. I don't care who you're with as long as you tell me; we're friends, we're supposed to tell each other stuff like this."

"I'm sorry I didn't tell you. It's just—" My mind searches for answers.

I flashback to the moment our relationship started. Back to December 7th right after Carmen's birthday fiasco. Ron got so mad that Carmen had not returned his feelings of affection. That's why he ran away from our friend Kat's apartment. Affection? Or lust?

I was dropping Ron off after hanging out with Carmen. I had parked behind the apartment's entrance. The car was silent; Ron was sitting right next to me in the passenger's seat. I was wondering why he didn't just leave right away. His left hand gravitated toward mine as his breathing became heavier.

"Can I do something real quick?"

"Wha—" my words were cut off as his face closed the gap between us in a surprise kiss.

I was in shock; I could barely move. I just sat there in disbelief as his lips formed kissing movements on my lips.

I finally regained feeling in my body as I broke the kiss.

"What are you doing?!"

"I thought you liked Carmen?"

"Why would you kiss me?"

"Because..." he sighed. "I like you too."

"But after Carmen turned me down, I knew my feelings for her weren't real. I just had a crush on her." I finally snap out of my flashback.

"Ron came to me. I didn't start our relationship."

"Wait seriously? He asked you out?"

"No, he kissed me first, and well, things kinda... went on... from there."

"Oh..." Carmen looked shocked.

"Have y'all had sex yet?"

"Pppppfft. No, I'm not ready yet."

"It's fine; we don't have to go into details, besides I know how big he is."

I smirk at her comment. She does too.

We sigh.

"It's not like I am going to let our relationship come between us. That only happens in TV shows and movies."

"Exactly," she agrees.

"You're both responsible adults, and I trust you to not let Ron come between us."

"I promise."

6

2020

My work shift starts at 6am. I am a Bagger at the local H-E-B. I work for $9.50 an hour; it isn't much, but it's honest work. The store closes early today for New Year's Eve. Even though it's a holiday, there are still last-minute shoppers finding their way to my line with 100+ items of wine, champagne, black-eyed peas, steak, bushels of grapes, poppers, sparklers—you know, the works.

I don't have a lot of friends at work, just acquaintances with name tags so I can't forget their names and so they can't forget mine, even when they want to.

Once my workday ends at 12 pm, I rush home with 72 gummy bears. I need 72 gummy bears for 72 Jello shots. I previously bought different five 99-travel size liquor bottles: prickly pear, pineapple, cherry limeade, grape, and green apple. I combined prickly pear 99 with lemonade and pineapple with orange Jello for flavor depth. I made cherry limeade, grape, and green apple with their corresponding Jello flavor.

"Look at this mess!" my mom comes into the kitchen with a broom. "Please tell me you are gonna clean up this mess, Adriana."

I finish up pouring the last batch of grape Jello shots into tiny cups.

"Yes, Mom, I am going to clean up."

I open the fridge to place my hoard of Jello shots when I see tall, crisp champagne-infused cake parfaits with strawberries and whipped cream in glass champagne flutes. My mom is an amazing cook and baker. She has her own cake selling business on the side, *Sylvia's Sweet Side*. Hopefully, I'll be as half a good cook as her when I move out.

I meticulously stack the cups upside down in a grocery bag in the fridge so that when you open a shot, it sticks to the lid and not the cup for easy shot access.

The party doesn't start till 8 pm, so I have time to spare. I wash the sticky, colorful residue from the pots, plates, and bowls I used and start to get ready.

I get dressed to the nines in my frequently complimented coral red formal shirt that flares at the sleeves. I put on my gold jewelry to accent my shirt and gold eye shadow. As I'm applying my makeup, I can hear fireworks go off in my neighborhood every so often, just so you don't forget it's New Year's Eve. I glance at my phone; it's 6:38. I'm ready, but I still have to pick up the boys before I head over to Carmen's Dad's house for the party.

I grab a red Jello shot and slide it into my throat.

"I'm almost out the door with my bag of Jello shots."

"Bye, Mom."

"You're leaving to Carmen's?"

"Yeah, the party is in spring."

"Ok, just make good decisions and don't come home intoxicated... okay?" She continues, "I trust you."

"Yes, Mom. Carmen said it was okay if we sleep over; there's a spare room."

"Are you sure it's okay? I can come pick you up."

"Yes, I'm sure, you can call her and ask."

"Alright then, be safe. Happy New Year."

"Happy New Year."

My dad says looking up from his TV. "Happy New Year, guys."

With all these shots, champagne, and whatever liquor her dad has, I know we will be spending the night, at least to sleep for two to three hours.

I pick up the boys in time for us to be on the road by 7:24, in my slick, white, beautifully caressing Toyota Corolla.

"Hey, guys, what's up."

Trent's hand appears from in between the seats. "Give."

I give my aux to Trent in the back since he demands it.

"I'm not gay for you Trent," Ron blurts.

"...I'm gay for Adri..."

Oh, Ron, he's such a tease, such a goofy one at that.

I'm on the Highway when I hear shuffling in the backseat.

"What's in the bag?" Trent asks dryly.

"Oh, just 71 Jello shots."

"Jesus."

"Damn, Adri," Ron looks at me in disbelief. "Are you trying to get the whole block buzzed?"

"Maybe." I giggle.

We finally arrive at Mr. Deleon's house. We park on the side of the house. It's a compact, cream-colored two-story home with a stone archway leading to the front door. There's a multitude of succulents and a giant monstera plant branching over the left side of the black front door. Ron knocks on the door, and we are greeted by Mike and Cadence, some mutual friends of Carmen.

"Hey, guys."

"Hey Mike." Ron steps in, and we follow suit.

Inside, the house is decorated with gold and silver helium balloons. A humble Christmas tree stands in the corner of the living room. The dining room table is covered with a black plastic table cover, adorned with gold and silver shining stars next to the golden plate chargers.

"Heyyyyy." Carmen appears from the kitchen to hug me. I hug the small of her back as her boobs press into me like they could leave an indent.

"Happy New Year!" I say into her breasts.

"Happy New Year, guys." Carmen looks from me to the boys.

"Happy New Year." Ron replies. Trent just looks at Carmen and smirks before hugging her.

"We're just finishing up the steaks."

As I walk into the kitchen, I glimpse Nigel cooking up some rib-eye steaks for everyone. He's a tall Hispanic man with square glasses and a huge crush on Carmen.

"Steaks will be ready in 5 minutes." The kitchen is bustling and aromatic with steak and shrimp aromas.

"Ey yo, Nige', can I get mine medium rare?" Ron eyes the steaks sizzling on the stove.

"I mean, if you need any help with those steaks, man, I gotchu." The movement of people inside the kitchen has me flustered for a spot to place my Jello shots.

"Bro." Nigel looks back at Ron. "All the steaks ARE medium rare, bro. Nah man, I got this."

"Oh, ok, nice dude."

I place the reusable grocery bag full of shots in the fridge. Carmen grabs a pan of shelled shrimp and places it on the table. I sit on the side closest to the front door next to Ron, opposite from Cadence. Mike, her boyfriend, sits next to her. Trent sits on the end to the right of Mike just outside the kitchen. There's only seven people in total, including me. It is an intimate dinner party.

Carmen rummages through her dad's liquor cabinet and pulls out bottles of red and white.

"Okay, Cabernet Sauvignon or Pinot Grigio?" He gestures with a bottle in each of his hands.

"Oooo how fancy..."

"I'll have the Pinot," Ron says, as she pours him a glass. Red wine is my favorite. "I'll have the Cabernet, please."

A stereo in the back starts playing "Living La Vida Loca" while Carmen fills everyone's glasses.

"Alright, guys, steaks are done! Come grab a plate!" Nigel announces from the kitchen.

We migrate one by one to the kitchen stove for our share, each of us coming out with our medium rare cuts in hand.

I crack open the fridge before heading back. "Hey, just letting y'all know I brought Jello shots for everyone in the fridge."

"Oh, nice," Mike turns around to look for a second and walks back to the table.

I start to close up the fridge, feeling proud of myself for making 72 Jello shots. Nigel grabs the fridge door mid-close.

"Oh, nice, lemme see," he grabs an orange one. "I'm guessing this is orange."

"Orange and Pineapple," I correct him.

"Ooooo, okay, bougie." He looks at me with a hurried expression, his voice turning into a whisper. "Adriana, you and Alice are close, right?"

"Yeahhhh... why?" The party-goers are served their steaks behind us at the stove.

"I need you to help me look good tonight." He adjusts his white collared shirt.

"Ummm, okay…"

"Please?"

"I want to impress Carmen tonight, so she'll like me more."

Nigel has always sort of been close to Carmen. He's always doing favors for her, like the one time he paid for her car repairs after she got into a car accident with her ex-boyfriend. Or when he helped her move into her new apartment. (This was before she had to move back in with her parents after the accident.) The point is, Nigel is always trying to be her knight in shining armor, riding on a white horse.

"I doubt it'll help." Nigel grabs another jello shot and swallows it whole, out of nervousness. "But I'll try." I take my seat at the table.

Carmen is the last to the table. She looks around, but all the seats are taken.

"Oh uhhhh..."

"Here, take my seat," Mike offers her his seat.

"Thanks, that's okay though, there is another chair here." She pulls a dining chair from the corner and sits between Mike and Trent, leaving Nigel to sit by himself at the end of the table.

Carmen places the wine in the middle of the table by a bowl of kettle chips as *Hotel California* by the *Eagles* plays quietly in the living room.

I look up at Nigel, who finishes his glass of wine as soon as Alice takes her seat. "Hey, Carmen, can you top me off?"

She stares at him, smiling. "More?"

"Yes. Pleeeaaase." Nigel tossed down his drink, leaving just a drop.

"Damn Nigel, okay," she remarks as she grabs the bottle. "Gonna finish all the wine?"

"Woooo, let's go Nigel." Mike pumps his fist in the air. Nigel chuckles as Carmen pours him another glass.

"Let's have a toast!" I declare to the guests.

"Yeah."

"You, ready?"

"Shhhh." Carmen quiets Cadence, who stops talking to Mike. They quiet to a murmur. The dining room is stunted with silence.

Nigel stands up. "Okay, everyone... Thank you all for coming tonight. It's been a hell of a year; hopefully, 2020 will give us the 2020 vision we need, so I don't have to wear these glasses anymore." His face turns into a frown and then back again into a tricky smile.

"We all laugh. "Nigel, you f***ing nerd," Ron calls out.

"Ron, you need 2020 vision too." I poke fun at him with his own glasses.

"Happy New Year, everyone."

"Happy New Year!" We all raise our glasses and say cheers as our glasses clink with one another.

"Cheers, babe." Ron and I clink our crystal glasses together.

"The food is sooo good, guys." Cadence is piling her plate with cocktail shrimps.

Ron stops me mid-chew. "Hey, did you bring a blunt.?" He whispers in my ear.

"No," I say with a mouthful. I don't carry weed on me.

"Hey, Hey Trent." He's talking to Carmen about different restaurants, and I can't hear all of it, but he mentions a bar.

"Trent."

"Sup?"

"Hey, did you bring the smoke?"

Trent just nods.

"Bet."

Carmen sees his head nod. "If you guys are going to smoke, go outside... please." Everyone starts to stare at us.

Carmen shifts in her seat. "My dad doesn't care if you guys smoke, just take it outside."

"Y'all finna smoke a joint. I brought smoke too." Mike looks at Cadence, who's opening her bag to reveal a paper joint.

"Hell, yeah man. Gotta hit it before dinner."

"Yessss...." Cadence follows behind the boys. They all eagerly leave their seats to smoke that good ol' reefer outside.

I'm not really into smoking. I just take CBD, which my parents want me to take so I don't end up on the streets addicted to Marijuana. Or some other inane idea they have about smoking weed.

I grab some chips and shelled shrimp from the table. The steaks are delicious paired with my red wine. The steak is so good I feel like I'm at a Michelin star restaurant, and the chef served up his last steak of the night, so he wasn't in a rush to sauté it. It's fresh and hot and marinated in juices; he was just glad the dinner rush was over.

"Mmmm..." the steak practically melts in my mouth.

"This is amazingly good, Nigel. What did you season it with?" I ask.

"Just good old salt, pepper, and a garlic and butter reduction."

"Wow, Nigel, you're a really good cook. Perfect husband material."

"Oh gosh, I don't know about that, but thank you." He blushes.

It's just me, Carmen, and Nigel at the table.

He looks at Carmen to see her reaction.

She shakes her head and furrows her brow.

"Ummmm, okay...." She says incredulously. She gets up. I get up to go follow the group. I walk around the kitchen stove and walk into the breakfast nook. She's peeking through the blinds to look at the smoke sesh outside.

Nigel follows me too.

We lift up the blinds on the patio to see the stoners sitting around a table smoking it up.

"Look at them, these adults have developed into highly sophisticated and deadly efficient devices of total destruction." Nigel points out.

"The crime club." Carmen adds.

"This is what our society has come to. This is the future the Democrats want." Nigel chuckles to himself.

"I'll not have my child smoking the devil's lettuce." I say in a southern accent.

Mike knocks on the window, and we lower the blinds.

"We'll be out in a second." Cadence's voice conforms.

I turn around, and I come back to my plate. Nigel pulls out his phone to look at Twitter news.

"Hmm, it says there is a mystery virus that's spreading throughout China."

"I thought it was supposed to be pneumonia?" Carmen questions the Twitter post.

"No, it's not. They are now saying it's this new viral disease, and China is now going on lockdown..."

The back door opens, and I catch a whiff of weed. Ron and Trent come back inside from their smoke session.

Dinner conversation goes on. Everyone is catching up on each other. Nigel tells everyone a story about his job working as an Assistant Manager for H-E-B curbside in Montrose in Houston. Some outlandish story about when he bagged groceries for Mike Strahan, the Texas NFL player.

"Yeah, I shook his hand as I gave him his groceries."

"His car, man... so nice, a Fiat."

Carmen stares at him curiously. "So, Mike Strahan, was he nice to you? Or was he rude to the staff?"

"No, nothing like that happened. He's a great guy. Told me I did a good job and tipped us 100 dollars."

"Sweet," our Mike raised his eyebrows and turned his mouth down with his lips pursed in approval.

"I just got a new job, and I put a down payment on a new one-story house in Porter."

Ron claps for them. "Wow, that's not bad at all, man! Very cheap for a house these days."

"Yeah, it's great. It's a two-bedroom, two-bath, one-story house. I just had to sell my kidney to afford it." He laughs jokingly. His eyes look down in buyer's remorse.

Laughter ensues.

After dinner is over, the group saunters over to the corner bar on the right side of the cream-colored house.

"I can make someone a mixer."

Ron perks up.

"Can you make me a Moscow mule?"

"Yeah, I can. I've got the mug for it and everything."

"Do you have lime?"

"Uh!" she shrugs her shoulders. "Duh, I am Mexican." We all laugh.

"I don't know what I want yet." I can only see a Ciroc and tequila at the bar, but there's a cupboard under the bar where more liquors are that are out of view. The smell of lime being squeezed punches my nose.

"Wait, actually, I change my mind."

"Oh. Okay."

"Let's take shots!" Ron looks at me.

"You wanna shot?"

"Yeah, I'll do shots with you."

"I can make buttery nipples." She holds the copper mug.

"Is anyone gonna take this Moscow mule?"

"I'll have it." Trent gets up from the grey quilt couch.

"Awww, everyone looks so cute, let's all take pictures." Carmen swoons.

As soon as she says pictures, Trent swivels on his right foot and heads back to the couch.

Carmen looks at him, offended. "Trent get over here... NOW." She stomps her foot.

"...ight."

Carmen pulls out her phone and snaps a pic of me in the middle of Trent and Ron.

"Cute. Come here, Trent, I want us to take one together."

She snaps a pic of her smiling underneath Trent, whose mouth is wide open and his tongue is out like he was a member of the band KISS.

"Okay, ready?" Ron asks me.

I look up. He's holding his buttery nipple.

"I've never actually had one before," I say with a smile.

"Ok, when you take a shot, you gotta drop it on the table... pick it up and swallow."

"Cheers!" We all raise our shots. Trent's deep voice adding an alto to our chorus.

I do what he tells me and chug the shot down. It's sweet and creamy.

One shot turns into two, and two turns into three.

"Want a beer to chase it down?" Ron holds up a Corona.

"Sure, I'll take one."

We all sit down around the rug in the living room.

"Here, lemme move the table."

Carmen moves the round, black coffee table (in front of the couch) so we can all sit around it.

On the backyard side of the room, there's a stereo with lights playing *Daft Punk's "Doin' It Right."*

I get up to move my hips to its electronic groove while Ron bobs his head next to me, standing up.

From the closet, Carmen pulls out her Astros-themed Jenga set. We sit around and chat while we move orange and navy blue blocks to the top of the tower. I lost the first round.

"These blocks are too smooth. It's harder than regular Jenga."

"That's the point. It's a challenge." Mike resets the tower.

"Once I'm done with this bottle, we should spin it," Nigel chugs straight up.

"NOOOOOO—!" Carmen chimes, "Gross." Cadence giggles.

I think about kissing other people here. I mean, it could be fun. I shake the idea out of my head... It's just the liquor talking...

The hour flies by as we play the game, just talking about anything. Workplace drama mostly; Carmen works the night shift at a hotel, so a lot of seedy and sexually needy people come to the hotel at night. I'm not offended, but she's been very disturbed by some of the people who walk in; some even carry guns... That's not okay, but we do live in a wooded area. You'd be surprised at what lurks out here in these woods...

When it's finally 11:32, we go outside to light fireworks on the driveway.

As soon as I step outside, the sound of the fireworks from the neighboring streets hits my ears, it is so loud my heart beats to their sound. Carmen begins to light the fuse of a fountain sparkler near the garage door, but before the sparkler goes off, Trent nudges her forcefully.

"Boo—"

"Aaaaaaa! Stop!" she pushes him back. I am starting to remember how Trent and Carmen used to date in high school. They would hold hands in the hallway as they passed by my locker during bell. She hates remembering high school though. A lot of the dark, nerdy types at school tried to use her. They would be called Incels nowadays. Not all of her boyfriends were Incels though. After she dated Trent, she was David's girl. He was 22 while she was 16. They were so in love, they almost moved in together. Carmen's mom wouldn't have it. Eventually, they would argue too much about money, and they eventually wouldn't work out. Carmen is single, headstrong, and independent; she makes her own money. She really doesn't need a man; she has us...

I stare blankly into the sparklers, showering lights.

"Hey, Adri, are you good?" Ron asks me, pulling me out of my memory. Ronnie always has my back.

"Yeah, I am fine." The sparks are now a dying flame.

We light up the rest of the night with wand sparklers and chase each other around with snappers, throwing and snapping them at each other's feet.

Snap "Ooowwwww!" Trent got me. I threw all my snappers at him in revenge. *Snap* *Snap* *Snap* * SNAP* "Heyyyy!"

"What... time is it?" Carmen asks out of breath.

"It's 11:57," Mike says looking up. We all return to the top of the driveway.

"Well... anyone want to say their New Years' resolutions?"

"Noooo," Trent shuts me down.

"I still need to fix my sink—" "Yeah, the sink," Mike and Cadence say, "I'm gonna lose weight." I look down at my large size shirt.

"NEW YEAR, NEW MEEE!" Carmen squeals in a snobbish high pitch.

"Woooo, That's right new year, new bitchh!" Cadence yells with her beer raised in the air.

The countdown starts "3... 2... 1!"

"HAPPY NEW YEAR!!" "Woooo!"

I grab Ron, and we spin around. "What are yo—"

"Hahah." We crash into each other; our lips collide to make sparks as we crash. I pull away and place my hand on his chest; his arms are around me. "Happy new year, Ron."

"Happy new year, Adriana." We come together in a hug. Mike lights his biggest firework in his arsenal. We watch the red and white colors flash in the air. The streets sound like a war-zone as the fireworks go off. I can feel the bass of the blasts in my chest, and in that moment, I swear I reach euphoria. I'm so grateful to have me and my closest friends to share my new year with. I'm seeing stars, or maybe just drunk. We end our firework show and step into the front entrance.

"Now that it's officially New Years, I say we should do more shots."

"Absolutely," Nigel wipes off his white dress shirt. "Damn, I think that one firework almo— Mike... Mike!"

"Huh? He's still halfway through the door pulling in the firework trash.

"You almost blew up my head, man."

Mike manages to make it to the kitchen. "Yeah, sorry about that Nigel." He steps behind the corner bar. "Carmen, is it alright if I pour everyone another shot?"

Carmen is on the couch with Trent; she looks ready to pass out. "Yeah, that's fine...." she sighs. "But I think this has gotta be the last one."

"It's no problem." Nigel pours the 1800 tequila. "Happy New Year everyone, let's make this year count." He starts the toast.

"Shietttt... I don't think I'mma be able to count after this shot."

"HA!" Carmen shouts before chugging her shot glass.

"You're f***ing stupid Ron." Trent snickers. I can't help but to laugh too. I drop my sixth shot down my throat. Soon I'm stepping all over the place.

"Whoa!" Ron holds me up. "You okay Adri?"

"Yeah." I manage to regain my balance on the hardwood floor. "Carmen, do you have any place to lay down?" I say as I'm reaching for a water bottle to stave off a hangover.

"Oh yeah, there's a spare room upstairs," Carmen says in her chest as she's cleaning off the bar. Mike and Cadence soon leave. They talked about how they have another party to go to.

"Bye, guys." They hug Carmen and Nigel before stepping outside.

"Bye." I wave at them from the stairway stoop. I make myself go upstairs; I am followed by Ron and Trent after Nigel leaves too.

"Adrienne!!" Ron yells in his Rocky Balboa accent. Like I haven't heard that one before. I smile to myself.

I play along. "Rockyyyyy...!" I giggle "I'm in the restroom!" I'm in the small bathroom connected to the spare room.

"I found it!"

"Found what?" I ask him, flushing the toilet.

"My wallet... It fell in between the couch cushions." Ron turns on the floor lamp by the bedside flooding the room with a warm glow.

"Oh, thank goodness." I comment as I wash my sweaty face in the bathroom. There isn't any makeup remover so I use hand soap to scrub my face. Anything is better than going to bed with makeup on. Carmen strolls into the room.

"Okay, we need to go to bed early so we can leave at 5 am."

"Early?" He scoffs. "Carmen... It's already 1:25 am."

"Well, we need to go to sleep as soon as possible. I have to go to work at 6, and I don't want anyone staying at my dad's place after I leave." Great.. I wanted to sleep in. Oh well. I dry my face with a yellow hand towel. Carmen, Ron, Trent, and I all try to fit in a queen-size bed.

"Okay, let's just sleep on the bed sideways. I'll set the alarm for 5 am." Carmen pulls out her phone. We awkwardly roll up the burgundy flower quilt to fit our bodies on the bed horizontally. Ron is fitted by the headboard as I squeeze next to him. I look to my right and Trent's next to me, then Carmen is at the end. I can feel my feet dangle off the edge of the bed.

"Hey scooch over." Ron pulls the covers up.

"I can't, Trent is right here."

"Stop moving me." I feel Trent's bony knee graze my leg. I'm glad it's dark; I can feel my cheeks burn red with embarrassment.

"Here I'll move." I hear Carmen's voice on the other side of Trent's body; she moves and then Trent moves as well so I can leave Ron room so he isn't pushed against me. A police siren goes off outside.

"How many people do you think got arrested in this neighborhood?" Ron asks the group fitted like sardines.

"I don't know, it's good Adriana's not driving tonight." I can smell beer on Trent's breath as he speaks.

"Guys, go to sleep; we only have three hours till we have to go on the road." Carmen whispers. The guys don't stop talking though. Instead, their voices turn to whispers. I fall asleep in a fetal position to the sound of their voices...

I'm jolted awake by Carmen's stupid alarm on her phone.

"Ughhh." I wipe the sweat off my forehead.

"I'm up, I'm up." Ron bolts up out of the bed to stretch.

"Carmen, turn it off." Trent pulls his pillow over his face.

We soon get up, and I hit the road with Trent and Ron. Carmen left in her car. I cruise down the highway towards home in my white Hyundai.

"You know you were talking in your sleep." Ron laughs.

"Yeah." Trent says snickering.

"What?" I laugh.

"Yeah, you were saying 'Who has my hamburger, I want a hamburger....' And then you just started mumbling in your sleep."

"That's hilarious. Did ya'll even sleep?"

"Barely, I probably slept for one hour."

We hop in my car and peel out into the darkness. As I am driving, I realize I can't go past 60 miles per hour without my steering wheel shaking and the car rattling. The waters I drank are finally starting to create equilibrium in my body. I finally make it off the highway and drop off Ron first and then Trent since he lives farther into Kingwood. I'm starting to get dizzy and severely nauseous. Oh god. My stomach drops, oh no... Not here, not now. I stop myself from throwing up. Please, just let me make it home. Once I'm finally near my subdivision, it's 40 mph here. Outside it's so dark except for the spotlights shining upon the Baptist church sign by the stop sign. I bear down on my steering wheel—I can roll down my window— and my stomach hitches and slams up at me. It's too slow. I open up my car door and immediately projectile vomit in the middle of the street.

This is so pathetic... I think to myself. I look around to see if there are other cars, but no one's around to see me. I let out a few more coughs and make myself purge whatever is left from my stomach. I wipe my face and close the car door.

That's it, I won't let alcohol get in my way this year. It's my last year; I have to graduate. I am graduating with my associate's degree. It's all or nothing this year.

7

How To Not Get Drafted

Today is a bright and windy day. It's Friday, January 3rd 2020. After the New Year's party, I put my car in the shop. It's too scary to let my car drive down the highway with a slightly crooked steering wheel, accompanied by a rattling sound down the highway. Not a chance.

Right now I'm looking out of Carmen's car window while *Zombie* by the *Cranberries* plays on the car radio. Trent is sitting in the front passenger next to Carmen who's navigating through traffic. Ron is sitting next to me, I lean into his shoulder every time the car makes a hard left turn.

"Im glad we're going to the Galleria mall instead of Greens point mall."

"Don't you mean Gunpoint mall?" Trent says looking at traffic.

"Yeah, it's scary over there, people got shot."

"Yeah, a woman who owned a lingerie store was held at gunpoint and shot in the head... Then he shot himself after removing her clothes."

"Whoa..." I look at him with eyes wide.

"Yeah... They still don't know why he did it." I lean into him for comfort.

"It's really scary in the city. Even outside the city, like when Hasan was held at gun point at the Gym parking lot in Porter." (Carmen is talking about her recent off-again on-again ex-boyfriend Hasan, they're just friends right now.)

"Yeah, I remember when that happened."

"It's like I can't even go to that gym anymore because of what happened to him."

She still goes to the same gym where the incident happened but now she only parks at the front and she has to go with someone all the time. We finally make it inside the Galleria mall. It's so large it needs three stories to fit all the expensive name brands like Gucci, BCBG maxima, Versace etc. The mall is so big it even holds an Ice rink. I still remember my first time skating on the ice rink when I was in girl scouts. We walk around the white marble floors to the left side of the 2nd floor.

"Oooooh, let's stop at H&M; I need new work clothes." Carmen points at the H&M store that takes up two stories.

We walk behind the glass and browse the immense collection of formal wear, I finally settle on trying on a denim overall dress and a black pencil skirt with a silver zipper having a large ring attached to it. For the top I picked out a white collared blouse with small hearts seamed in across the blouse. It looks good on me, besides Valentine's day is coming up. The dress and the skirt did not do me any favors and looked stretched over my chubby body. I hop out of the curtained dressing room. I place my unwanted clothes on the rack. I come back to the white tables of folded clothes I spot a really nice peach colored sweatshirt.

"What did you get?" Carmen meets me at the cash register.

"The white blouse and this peach sweatshirt."

I pay for my clothes "You didn't get the skirt? But it looked so cute on you." Tell that to my hips.

"No, it was too short."

Ron pops out from the men's section at the top of the marble stairs. "Hey, Adri look what I found." He holds out a black cap with a gold band across the front just like Jotaro Kujo from season three of Jojo's Bizarre adventure, a popular fighting anime. Me and Ron are both obsessed with him.

"Guys.. guys," we all look at Trent who's reading from his phone. "The Pentagon just confirmed an American strike killed Iran's Supreme Leader." A few people stop to turn their heads. I look at them walking over the cold white marble tile and offer them an awkward smile.

"Holy shit." Ron sounds shocked gawking at the headline on Trent's phone.

"No way..." I exclaim.

"There's now a Twitter hashtag: #WorldWarThree. Everyone's talking about how we're gonna get drafted."

"What?!" That's awful. I don't want to go to war. This has to be a joke, right? "Women can't get drafted I know that. I KNOW we aren't going to get drafted. Would you go to war?" Carmen adjusts her shopping bag on her shoulder.

"Hell no, War is hell." Ron steps up to the cashier to buy his pants.

"I would go to war." Trent smiles down on Carmen.

"Wha—"

"No you would not. You wouldn't last a week in combat." Carmen pushes him. He laughs.

"Not with them skinny jeans." I jeer.

"Uh, Shut up....Stop body shaming me." Trent looks down at me through his nose.

"Yeah, Adriana." Carmen laughs.

"UGH, Yeaahhhhhh." Trent retorts in a valley girl high pitched voice with his hands on his hips.

The guys get bored of shopping, nothing really interests them. So we make a few more stops to Urban Outfitters (found nothing there, it was all too expensive.) Lush, Hot topic etc.

"Are you hungry?" Ron looks at me.

"No, not really." I say looking at a small Thai food restaurant. I will be later though.

"Let's not eat here, the food doesn't look good here. I know a spot that's close by." Carmen leads the way towards the mall exit.

Carmen takes the wheel and drives us toward an authentic ramen bar downtown. Where they actually cooked and served Ramen right in front of you. They served our noodles in bright red, ornate bowls.

"This soup is fantastic. Mmmmm. Thank you." Ron complements the Asian man behind the bar before slurping up an egg noodle.

"I don't know the noodles aren't that good here. I've had better ramen." Carmen spins her ceramic spoon around in her half full bowl.

"That's because you ordered the vegan tofu ramen." Trent groans.

"Here have some." She accepts and Trent pours some of his bowl into hers.

"mmmm... Yours is so delicious, and spicy. Hoh hoh ho— Haaaaa!" She fans her mouth before downing her glass of ice water.

Trent chuckles to himself.

We finish up our meals, tip the server, drop Trent off and spend the rest of the night in the comforter in

Carmen's bed, watching videos and listening to music. It's so cozy here on her bed on the floor in her white comforter. I love when we have sleepovers like this, everything seems so perfect. It's like I can experience a part of my childhood once again (but with alcohol) before we become adults and get married and have full time jobs. Carmen is sitting up looking for a movie on Netflix for us to watch.

After I'm done scaring myself about World war three on my phone, I turn on the light.

"Hey! I want it to be dark!" Carmen squints.

"Hold on, I wanna show ya'll something." I pull out a whiteboard and marker from Carmen's shelf and title a list:

How To Not Get Drafted.

1. If you're Mennonite, Jehovah's Witness or Amish.
2. If you have a health condition.
3. If you're in college.
4. If you're a single parent male or female.
5. If you have face or hand tattoos.
6. If you have an essential civilian job.
7. If you've been previously enlisted in the army.
8. If you're pregnant.
9. If you're obese.
10. If you have any disability (even mental health issues).

I flip my board over to show the group.

"This is what you wanted to show us?" Carmen asks with a smile on her face.

"Alright so everyone do drugs, be gay and get pregnant." Ron declares. We all laugh.

"And in that order." Carmen laughs.

"Sorry Adri, I am... Im..." Ron snuffles a fake sob. "gay for Trent."

We laugh even harder.

All of a sudden, someone knocks on the door.

"Who is it?" Carmen yells.

"It's me." Stella, Carmen's youngest sister is at the door.

"I need to use your microwave," she asks sheepishly.

"Go use the oven downstairs." Carmen groans.

"The oven is broken, Martin broke it remember?"

"Uhhhhhh... " Carmen gets up from her Netflix scrolling to open the door.

Stella steps in. Her silhouette illuminated in the dark by the TV. She's petite with long wavy black hair. She has black shorts and a light gray sweater.

"I just need a few minutes."

She pops in her cup of macaroni in the microwave atop the silver mini fridge. In the corner wall by the wall divider. She crouches down in the corner, she appears so small and beggared, holding her bare knees by the mini fridge next to the wall dividing the toilet.

Carmen pulls out her phone as she tries to contain her laughter. She starts to record her sister with the flash on.

"Nooo Staahhhp!" Stella holds her small hand up to block her face but now we are all laughing at her.

"You're so ruuudee." She says covering her face.

"The struggle." Carmen says, putting her on full blast.

"Leave her alone she just wants to nuke her mac and cheese." Ron gags.

"Plea he heaseee..." Stella begs.

"I'm just a struggling artist."

We laugh at her depreciation

"I can't afford fancy ramen in the city." She says under a tight lipped smile. Luna, Carmen's heavily pregnant cat, comes over to investigate Stella.

Stella doesn't have a job but she's an amazing digital artist. I've seen her draw amazing sunsets and landscapes on her tablet for money. But she's actually planning on going to A&M for college to become a veterinarian.

"It's just macaroni..." she huffs.

"God." Stella grabs her cup and leaves.

"She always has to be in my business." Carmen sighs and flops back on her bed.

This time we just settle on picking YouTube music videos. Ron stays up talking to Carmen, as Luna slinks over to me and rubs her head into my face before curling up in a ball.

"I think Luna likes youuuu." Ron coos.

Carmen tilts her head to peer at Luna curled up by my head.

"Oh, she's been acting like that ever since she got pregnant."

I still think it's because she likes me, even though I'm terribly allergic.

I fall asleep to the sound of Alt-Psychedelic music and the sound of Luna purring.

***

"Hey guys, wake up, I have to go to work." Carmen wakes me from my deep slumber.

"Nooooo." I roll over like a burrito in her covers.

"Ugh, guys I have to leave." She says while doing make up in her bathroom mirror. The yellow, blinding light from the bathroom irritates me as I'm slowly forced to wake up.

We eventually back out of Carmen's driveway. I stare wistfully at the misty Meadows on the way home before we drive by the houses again. Something seems off about Carmen. She seems easily irritated, more than usual.

It's 8:58, I get home and nap before I have to drag myself to work. A message lights up my phone on my pillow.

Carmen: When do you wanna chill? I'm gonna go eat and go jogging real quick. Oh right you work till 4. :/

Me: Ye

I close up my phone and head to work. Its business as usual. I buy a prepackaged salad and an Arizona tea. The same thing I get every time for my lunch break. I check my phone an hour before I get off work at 5:07

Carmen: so we not hanging out?

Me: What about the 7th? I'm off that day.

Carmen: Okay I'm off that day.

I head home in my sisters white Malibu since my car is still in the shop. I go to college on Wednesday the 5th. To study After effects, I have to edit myself in front of a green screen getting hit by a red car. I use the garbage bag method to mask out a rough shape of me in front of green screen so I can Photoshop the area around the car to make it look like I'm getting struck by a car and doing a cartwheel after being hit. After effects isn't as hard as I thought, you just have to follow the Professor step by step and there's at least 32 different steps on the After Effects Adobe software. It's easier than code that's for sure.

The next day, at 8pm, my dad gets the call informing him that my car is finally ready. He took it to the city to get it fixed by this guy who fixes cars from his own garage. I open my phone to tell Carmen the good news.

Me: Hey I got my car back from the shop!

Carmen: Ooo Yay! Luna's about to give birth

Me: Oooooo call me when she does

Is it cool if I come over to see?

Carmen: Hasan Is here

Me: Oh okay...

Carmen: You can come see the kittens tonight probably. Just late if that's ok. Idk If it's gonna take her forever so...

Me: yeah that's okay

I come over to find that Luna isn't giving birth quite yet.

She's in a box making a nest for her babies, kneading and pressing down on marvel themed cotton blankets. It's amazing how her natural instinct prepares her for the birth.

"She hasn't started yet, but she started but she's making bed." Hasan looks down at her. He's a very handsome Muslim man, skinny too. But he's been known to get clingy. especially toward Carmen. Like for instance, when he made threats to almost every guy she dated after they broke up.

"I know! She keeps trying to make a nest in the attic behind the bathroom." Carmen points to the bare wood rafters on the far side of the bathroom.

"I had to get my dad to get her out. And he covered the hole with a piece of wood. So she can't go back there anymore." she says it like she's out of breath.

"We got her this box though, she seems fine now."

I look at the box covered by a blue floral sheet. Luna mews at her voice saying her name, and seems to be almost panting like a dog.

I leave her house and try to fall asleep, dreaming of her cute little grey and white kittens. Before I could reach REM sleep I'm woken up by my phone going off.

Carmen: Hey are you up

Me: Yes

Carmen: Ik it's late af but would ya'll be down to hangout for a little? I'm really depressed I didn't want to tell you guys that day I dropped ya'll off. My friend passed away.

Me: Oh :((Who?? Is it happening.

Carmen: Yeah I've been a mess I had to leave work Andrew, you didn't know him

Me: Oh noooooo

Carmen: I just saw him the other day too

Me: BB

Carmen: But yeah idk if you're not tired I would love the company. Me: Do you want me to bring Ron?

Carmen: Trent is up too yeah ya'll can all come I'm asking him tho

Me: Alright bet

I get up and change out of my pajamas and make my way toward Trent since he's the farthest from Carmen at the back of Kingwood. I look at my phone at a stop light.

Carmen: He said yes is Ron with you

Me: No I'm on my way to pickup Trent

Carmen: bet I'll let him know

I finally arrive with the crew at Carmen's house.

"Hey, guys thanks for coming."

"No problem." Ron steps over her pile of laundry.

"Yeah it's been really tough since my friend, Andrew passed away."

I knew something was wrong with Carmen, she needs her friends to be with her now. Trent stands over her bed. "So, do you want to tell me...?" we all look at him in suspense. "...How your friend died?"

"Trent! What if she doesn't want to talk about it?" I scold him.

"It's fine Adriana... He was riding his motorcycle when he got into an accident with an 18-wheeler." She sighs.

"Dang."

"Oh god!" My hands go up to cover my mouth in shock. "That's awful."

"I just saw him the other day too, I... I jus— I can't believe he's...," a small tear escapes her eye.

"Come here." I give her hug and rub her back. she sniffles into my shoulder.

"He's in a better place now." I comfort her.

Ron comes over and pulls something out of his pocket.

"Here, you need this." He hands Carmen a small sandwich bag of green bunches of weed.

She sniffles. "Thanks?" She says with a question in her voice. like somehow weed is going to fix everything. like somehow weed bring Andrew back.

Carmen wipes her tears from her face. "Here, Let's use my pipe." Carmen pulls out her Sublime themed weed tray underneath her coffee table. We all sit down in a circle on the floor like Native Americans passing the peace pipe. Ron grinds the kush up for her. He has to grind it twice to make the leaves small enough for Carmen to fit in her marbled purple glass pipe.

"Okay let's all go outside to smoke it. I don't want my mom to smell weed through the air vents." "I've never actually smoked in my room, my worst fear is my mom finding out I smoke by smelling it through the vents."

Luna meows loud at us and gets up, but decides not to, and curls up in a ball again.

We get situated on the two story porch. "She's not ready to give birth yet. I wanna be here when she does though." Carmen takes the first hit from the bowl and exhales it into the night air.

She hands me the pipe I light up the purple and aquamarine bowl. Inhale... hold and expel smoke from my mouth and simultaneously inhaling it through my nose in a french inhale.

A few minutes later and my head is swimming and I'm happy I feel high. Maybe Ron is right, marijuana does cure depression.

"Guys we should do something. lets go somewhere..." "Sure." Ron's turn to light the pipe.

"We need to get out. We should go to Las Vegas."

"I'd be down." Trent sucks on his vape

"I don't know about that one, chief." Ron discloses.

"It's true, Las Vegas is pretty far." I look at Carmen.

She's on her phone already looking at flights to Nevada on her phone while leaning against the rail keeping her from falling 1 story down. "Come on. Please!" Carmen begs.

"You come on. I don't have money for plane tickets. I wanna go somewhere we can drive to."

She stops arguing and stares blankly at me, thinking of possible destinations.

"What if we went to Florida? Ya know, stay on the beach, maybe go to Universal studios."

"Hmmm... maybe."

"Stop it Carmen, just make up your mind! We can't drive all the way to Florida. We would have to sleep on the road and I'm not sleeping off a feeder road in a car waiting to get robbed and murdered."

"We can book a cheap hotel midway. I don't see the big deal."

"What if we just went to Austin." I gesture to her.

"We could... We could use my hotel discount to stay at a hotel for the night. "

"Oh my gosh that would be so fun."

"And we could visit SoCo and have drinks on 6th street." We hug each other.

"You need get out, Just get your mind off what happened." I console as I break our hug.

"Yeah okay, but we have to save up for the trip."

Ron tosses his hair back. "Yeah, and it's only a three hour drive."

"We can take my car now that it's fixed."

Trent grins "Great, Sounds like a plan."

I go to drop off Trent at his place first so Ron and I can be alone together before I drop him off. I pull up to the sheltered parking lot in his apartment complex.

"Wait. let's not park here. The lights are too bright. Someone will see us. Park over there." He points to the far left side of the parking lot where the lights are out.

I do as I'm told before striping down to please him. We make out in my backseat. One thing leads to another and I lean in and crush into him over and over until he moans in my ear and finishes in my mouth.

"Here let me get you some water." He clothes his nakedness and disappears behind the small fence and comes back with two water bottles.

"Thanks Ron."

"Yeah no problem. Hydration is important." he kisses me.

"Bye Adri. Text me when you get home, okay?"

"Bye Ron."

I put my keys into ignition and start my engine. I'll probably forget to text Ron back. It's late and I just want to pass out at this point. I back out of the parking spot and as soon as I reverse I accidentally scrape the side of my car on the concrete pole.

"Shit!" I step out onto the hard cracked concrete to inspect the damage. It left a brown dent on my cabin door, the scratch reminded me of the stretch marks on my thighs.

"What the f**k!" I just got my car out of the shop too.

I go home pissed after our hangout. I crash into my bed and think about Carnen's dead friend. She isn't going to his funeral. It's for his family mostly, but she hates funerals anyway. Too many sad people, and Carmen hates being sad. I wake up and get ready for my portfolio class, I have to create my own Logo and Business card to graduate in multimedia design. It's like graphic design except I have to take animation, web design and Video classes. I think back to the 'How not to get drafted' list I made. Heh, I'm in college so even if I was a man I wouldn't get drafted because I'd be in College, learning how to do something I can find out on you tube.

8

Karaoke night

I check my phone as soon as the professor is done with the lecture.

Carmen: "What time are you done with school?"

Me: "Right now."

Carmen: "Do you want to go to the gym or to the park? And we can plan out the trip too."

Me: "Maybe. What about if we went to China town? We can finally do karaoke. When did you want me and Ron to come over?" I text as I make my way to Trent's place.

Carmen: "Well, Luna's not showing signs yet, and my sis will check on her."

Me: "Oh, okay. Ugh, I hate having to meet up with Ron at his place. I scraped my car coming out of his parking lot last night."

Carmen: "Oh no, that sucks. Ya'll can't hang out at your place or his, Lmao?"

Me: "Mmmm, my parents hate him."

Carmen: "Did he not talk to them?"

Me: "Carmeeeeeeen." I'm haunted by my dad yelling at me for sneaking Ron in to stay over that one night.

Carmen: "My mom doesn't want people at my place when I am gone."

Me: "Oh."

Carmen: "Did he not talk to them?"

Me: "No."

Carmen: "Are they not going to? What happened?"

Me: "Who? What?"

Carmen: "I mean, you said they hate him, did he not talk to them like you said they wanted him to?"

Me: "Ohhhhh, yeah, they haven't talked to him."

Carmen: "Why do they hate him then? Lol, tell him they should talk to them."

Me: "F**k."

Carmen: "Are you embarrassed? Lol." I am a little embarrassed.

Trent is in my backseat when Ron steps in, absolutely drenched in cologne. "Hey babe." We kiss.

"Ugh." I can see Trent roll his eyes in my rear-view mirror.

"Oh, are you afraid of intimacy Trent?" I ask him playfully.

"No, just you two."

"Quick Adri, play some U2." Ron snickers.

"Just shut up and give me the aux." I give him my cord, and he floods my stereo with the band KISS- "I Was Made for Lovin' You."

I get to the front of Kingwood to pick up Carmen. She's dressed in a sheer short sleeve shirt and a black camisole with plum-colored lipstick. Is she dressed Goth or in mourning? I can't tell... I just really hope this time she spends with us makes her feel better. She deserves to be consoled during the wake of Andrew's death. Carmen hops in next to Trent in the backseat.

I escape the dense forest that is Kingwood and commit to the hour-long journey to China town in Bellaire, south of Houston. We find a parking spot in the middle of the plaza. We walk around to the far side of the plaza, but closed signs were placed at the front of several shops.

"Why are so many places closed?" I ask.

"Yeah, this spot was open last time I was here." Carmen looks into an empty authentic Chinese restaurant.

"It's because of COVID-19," Trent states.

"Yeah, it's spreading in China. A lot of people are suffering right now in China. That's probably why they're closed. They had a lot of their supply chains shut down in China," Ron discloses while he looks down at the sidewalk.

I look at him. "Damn, that's terrible."

"Yeah, hopefully, it doesn't come to the U.S." Carmen steps away from the closed shops. We walk closer to the middle of the plaza.

"Let's go upstairs... Look!" She points to the building in the middle of Chinatown. "I can see an open sign." The bright red neon sign flashes on the second-story building made of brick and concrete. The place is called Neway Restaurant & Lounge.

We climb the concrete stairs to a lively lounge tucked away upstairs. We step into the door, and a wind chime sounds our arrival. I'm surrounded by neon blue lights and cascading crystal chandeliers as we enter Neway, on Dun Huang Plaza, 2nd Floor, Unit D23. We looked all around Chinatown for a good place to eat, but surprisingly, a lot of family-owned Asian places Alice wanted to go to were closed due to the growing threat of Covid 19 in China. So we decided to try something new and climbed up the concrete stairs to get to Neway. Neon blue LED lights lit up all the way to the bar on the left, to the overhead half-moon frames on the right. Lucky bamboo plants and crocus flourished in the back beside a small stage. A stage complete with a TV and a karaoke machine.

"Ooo look, in the back there's a karaoke machine."

"No. I'm not doing that." Trent bemoans.

Two drinks later...

Trent is atop the stage singing "Superstition" with Ron. I whip out my phone to capture the performance. Ron is going all out with his vocals. As he sings, he's lightened from behind as the lines of blue and green neon lights glow on the wall behind him and Trent. Ron even points at me when he sees me recording, while Trent quickly backs out of my camera shot. I look back at Carmen.

"Woooooo!" The lights flash behind them.

"Let's go Ron—Oow!" I yell out for their duo like a crazed fan. There isn't anyone in the restaurant. I only see just one wayward soul just getting off work to have a couple of drinks at his favorite watering hole.

Once they're done with their song, Carmen grabs my arm.

"Come on."

"No, no, I just wanna drink." I hover over my seat at the booth.

She giggles. "Come on, there's no one here." She tugs on my arm even more.

"Okay. Fineee." We stand upon the small stage (it was more like a platform) as she flips through the song book on the pedestal.

She finally lands on a song she likes. "Ooo—" she points to the laminated pages of the song book. "Let's do Abba- Gimmie Gimmie."

Of course, it is her favorite Abba song. I muster the song from the bottom of my chest, and we sing Abba word for word. I stare out at the boys sitting in the booth, watching us. I sing the best I can; I listen to the words and maybe... I am looking for a man every midnight. I glance at Ron, who's smiling and clapping. He puts his hands around his mouth like he's yelling into a loudspeaker.

"Wooooo Adri!" He cheers, and Trent drinks his martini in the dark blue leather booth. I smile at Ron. While I'm on stage, I think about our own escapades at night and how Ron has actually surprised me with his lovemaking. The way he goes down on me is the best feeling ever. And yet, I don't know if I see us going anywhere in this relationship. My stare becomes blank. What are we doing together?

"Gimmie, gimmie, a man after midnight." "Won't somebody help me chase the shadows away." I'm illuminated by the lights behind us as we stand on the platform. I look at Carmen as the light catches her hair, illuminating her, giving her a blue halo of light when we sing. Maybe my love life will finally make sense with Ron.

Once our Abba cover is over, we unceremoniously make our way to the exit.

"I'm starving." I look at Carmen and Ron behind me as I exit stage left.

"Come on, guys, let's go to Tiger Den before they close." Carmen steps in front of us to lead the way. She's been to Chinatown and Tiger Den many times before, so we trust her navigation. We follow Carmen downstairs to a little, hidden-away ramen restaurant. It's a cozy and bustling establishment, with warm glowing lamps hanging from the ceiling and dark wood paneling covering the wall at the entrance. I look to the right and see a modern Japanese city mural with a TV playing spots overhead.

"Table of 4, please." Carmen tells the host. While we wait to be seated, I stare at a panel at the front layered with dozens of drawings and doodles on napkins made by different creative customers. I peep at the drawings, like Marvin the Martian or Naruto, random memes, signatures, and doodles. A kind Asian waiter comes up to us and asks; "Table or booth?" She nods at us. We all look at each other.

"Booth," Ron tells her as we make our way to follow her.

The restaurant is divided into three seating sections. She seats us at a booth on the right and hands us four black menus. I sit next to Ron inside the booth, across from Carmen. We all order waters while Trent orders a Japanese beer.

"Hmmm." I open the menu and browse the five pictures of Ramen:

- Tonkotsu 8.00

- Garlic black bean 8.00

- Miso 9.00

- Spicy miso 9.00

- Tantan-men 9.00

I flip to the other side. I read the description at the top. Yakitori: "Yakitori" literally means "grilled bird" and traditionally consisted only of various parts of chicken. But in modern usage in Japan, it refers to any sort of chicken, beef, pork, seafood, and vegetables on skewers, "kushi" grilled on charcoal. Two skewers per order.

I decide on the Tonkotsu: The original silky "Tonkotsu" (pork) noodle soup topped with chashu, ajitsuke tamago, menma, cabbage, kikurage mushroom, scallion, fresh garlic. While I browse my menu, Carmen and Trent do so too.

"That looks really good." Carmen holds up her menu and points.

Trent looks over to see her menu. "It does."

Once the waiter arrives, everyone orders. Carmen orders the spicy miso ramen, and so does Trent. Ron and I are going to be splitting a bowl of Tonkotsu ramen since I'm buying; since he doesn't work. I also order the octopus yakitori.

"It's crazy how these days have just flown by," I say, passing my menu to the waiter.

"I know, right?" Carmen agrees while giving her menu back.

"It has been going so fast; it feels like a Friday." I squeeze my lemon into my water and stir the glass.

"This place has a great atmosphere." Carmen sips her water. "I've been here with Hassan so many times."

"I'm glad Tiger Den is still open." Ron leans back into his seat. "A lot of Asian places are struggling right now."

Our food arrived in a fast and timely manner. Steaming hot bowls of some of the best ramen in Houston (or so I've heard) are placed in front of us.

"Oh, excuse me." Carmen stops the waiter.

"Yes, ma'am." The waiter turns around.

"Can I get a plate of the takoyaki and the grilled brussel sprouts, please?"

"Right away, ma'am."

"And I'll have a water." Trent adds.

"Of course, it'll be right out."

"Thank you."

We indulge in the savory noodles, chock full of nutritious vegetables and meat. The dish is so hot; steam fogs up my glasses. As Ron and I finish halfway through our bowl, the waiter arrives with two plates of appetizers and my yakitori. The octopus is dark pink and grilled to perfection. I look over to Carmen; her plate of takoyaki balls is hot, and the brussel sprouts are blackened.

"These are so good; I get the brussel sprouts every time I come here. Adriana, you have to try some." She places the vegetable on my rectangular plate; it's dripping with sauce. In reality, I hate brussel sprouts with a passion. I always have. They taste like a smelly fart. I always see them at the table when my family has Thanksgiving; everyone has them on their plate except for me.

So when I stare at the brussel fiend on my plate this time, I am extremely wary of it. I pluck at the plant on my plate.

"Come on, try it. It's good."

I peel a leaf from the sprout and stick the single leaf on my tongue and chew.

I am shocked, absolutely gobsmacked. "Oh wow." I grab the whole piece and shove it into my mouth like I loved brussel sprouts. "This is the best brussel sprouts I've ever tasted!"

"See, I told you."

We finish our delectable meal and pay our separate tabs, plus tip. We stroll out of the restaurant with full bellies and walk to the opposite side of the plaza to window shop all the cutesy little pink Japanese makeup and accessory stores. I spot a boba tea shop and stop in for some green tea with boba. God, I love boba.

"I want to go to a real karaoke room, like an actual Japanese room where we can do karaoke in privacy." Carmen takes out her phone to look for any local karaoke spots on her phone.

"Hmm, I don't see any around here. We might have to drive to the other si— found it! There is one right here on this side, wait." She stops and scrolls with her mouth slightly open in concentration. "Oh, it's upstairs over here—" she points further down the lane to the staircase. Right above the Star Ice and the teriyaki store, there's a neon sign that says Yes KTV and a big decal on the glass window that says Karaoke room.

We enter, on the left side there's a glass top bar with alternating red and orange swivel seats. Overhead the bar, tiny overhanging lamps dangle on wires. Paneled mirrors behind the bar and concession stand reflect our arrival. A woman with a surgical mask greets us. "Hi, welcome to Yes KTV."

Carmen steps up to the lady behind a cash register. "Hiii can we get a karaoke room for four people?"

"Sure, here are the room rates—." She taps on a paper list taped to a glass box in front of the cash register.

Carmen and Ron read the room rates as I peruse the snacks inside the glass counter. The snacks are about the same as the snacks you buy at a movie theater. They're almost as overpriced as theater snacks too.

"Let's take the first one, the Mini room."

"Alright. Let's go, fam."

The room is red-orange with neon orange lights illuminating the ceiling in bright tangerine colors. I look down. In the middle of the room, ornate square glass coffee tables emanate pink neon lights. There's a large flat screen TV hanging on the wall next to the door. On the other side, two-toned leather couches take up the left corner of the room. The Karaoke machine (looks more like a computer screen) sits on the right side of the TV screen.

I lay back on the couch, Ron takes his spot next to me. Trent casually slouches next to him. And Carmen sits in the rolling stool next to the computer screen so she can be in charge of the song choice.

The host hands us all wireless microphones before they leave. The boys pick the first song; it just so happens to be Michael Jackson's "Beat It." They start grooving and head-bobbing to the intense bell chimes when the song starts. Even Trent is grooving to the beat (a rare sight), with his eyes closed and his eyebrows furrowed. He pumps his hand holding the mic to the beat of the song; "Beat it."

It's fun to watch the boys sing. They get into the spirit of Michael Jackson. I mean really get into it; they even perform half-decent moonwalks between verses.

Carmen plops down in front of the karaoke controls as soon as the song is over. "Okay, I get to pick the next song." She taps a few times on the touch screen, and a drawn-out beat plays through the speakers as "Kiss Me Thru the Phone" starts to play.

"Ohhhhhh Yeah! This is my jam! I went hard to this song in middle school." Ron puts his mic to his mouth like he was Soulja Boy himself and sings the lyrics without even reading the screen. The cellular beep-bop of the song takes control, making us pop and lock and move our hips to every 'Miss you, I just wanna kiss you.' I sing to the chorus as the night goes on.

We sing "Carry on My Wayward Son" by Kansas. The boys take a break and sit down while Carmen and I sing her favorite song; "Just Give Me a Reason" by Pink plays. We then sing the best song of all time, "Bohemian Rhapsody." I attempt to hit the highest notes of the song but fail. To keep the vibes going, I choose the next song.

"What are you going to pick, Adri?" Carmen calls out from the couch.

"It's a surprise."

"No, seriously, what is it so I can prep— Ohhhhhh." She warms up her vocals.

"Okay," I finally find my selection on the catalog and hit play.

"What is i—" a record scratch interrupts Carmen. "Oh my goddddd!"

"I still hear your voice when you sleep next to me..." I sing as I reach my hand out to Carmen.

"Your boyfriend's over there," she points to the left and laughs.

I look at Ron as he realizes and gets up from his seat.

"YEAH! LET'S GO!"

I grab the mic and stomp my foot on the coffee table.

"WITHOUT YOU, IT'S HARD TO SURVIVEEEEEE!"

Everyone's singing "Every Time We Touch" by Cascada. As I look around, everybody is getting down and rocking their hips and jumping to the electronic bass drop. I look to my left and see a flash of black hair; it's Trent, who's headbanging like he's at a Korn concert.

Like a cinema in my head, I'm all at once taken back to my middle school dance. Everyone was hot and sweaty. They promised us pizza, but all you got was half a slice of pizza and one small plastic cup of coke or grape soda. I didn't care if no one asked me to the dance. I was with my friends, dressed up in '80s themed

Justice brand clothes. We weren't obsessed with buying $200 dresses; we just danced, jumping out of control in a circle to this song. We lost our middle-school minds that night, dancing to the top 2010s songs and swinging and sliding through bounce houses during the slow songs.

I snap back to reality once the song is over. The karaoke machine turns on its Yes KTV screensaver.

"Ope, looks like our time's up," Ron says out of breath.

Trent wipes the sweat off his head. "Alright, let's skeedaddle."

We leave a tip for the host and vacate the room, leaving behind the echo of our songs.

9

Latin X Lives Matter

When work ends and college is over for the week, Carmen takes us to her favorite hangout spot in Houston: The Axel Rad beer garden. Once we get to the bar, we turn the corner.

"Holy shit! Look!" Ron points to it. On a random building next to the bar is a black-and-white sign. It shows the face of a person in power repeated, copied over and over, with their mouth freakishly wide open, eating the words… ENJOY THE COLLAPSE.

"What the f***." I gasp. "Who did this?"

"I don't know, but look, it says… ICE in the corner." Ron strains to look while driving. He parks the car in a nearby parking lot.

The place looks unsuspecting on the outside, just a red brick town building with white window trim. Once we step inside the bar, the appeal becomes obvious. The artsy but also modern decor offers us a fresh and hip entrance. White paneling on the inside appears as we walk in, with benches along the paneled wall stacked with colorful geometric pillows. Above the bench is a bookshelf next to hanging plastic ivy vines. The bar sits on the right side; further down the right is a jewel blue photo booth, its light glowing from the inside. The sounds of hustle and bustle escape the kitchen doors.

The bar isn't crowded; a few people are seated at crisp white tables in the center of the room.

"I'm gonna get us a drink." Carmen looks at us and points a thumbs up to the bar. "You know there are seats outside, too."

"Oh okay... let's—" Ron mumbles to himself, more in awe at the place around him. We step outside through the six-paneled French door to the outside, and it's like a whole another world.

It's an enormous backyard that's open to the public. A crate myrtle tree is adorned with strips of neon lights that glow different colors. It's a simple but awesome light show.

"Woah." I look around. It's like a hippie's backyard. On the right, there are groups of rainbow hammock chairs with small bright-colored iron side tables next to each hammock.

It felt as if a carnival was taking place. Hanging lights were strung up overhead the hammocks. I sat down at a picnic table to absorb it all.

"Adri! We're over here!" Ron calls out to me from the Hammock chairs. He props up on one of the vinyl lawn chairs in our group of hammock chairs while

Trent slumps back onto a beige hammock. "Mmmmmm." He sighs as he sets his giant shoes on the round, woven coffee table.

I slowly sit back into the Hammock chair next to Ron. I stop to listen to the sound of Reggae and R&B in the distance.

"This is really nice." I look at Ron.

"Have you been here before?" He asks me.

"No, this is my first time."

"Yeah, it's pretty great here. Sometimes, they do live shows and have food trucks."

"Really? Wow."

"Yeah."

We relax in the chairs for a while; the strings of lights above send warm light over all of us, and a late winter breeze cools us down. I debate on whether I should join Carmen and buy a drink...

"Do you guys know what drinks they serve?"

"Hmmm, I'm pretty sure they have basic beer here, like Corona and Bud Lights or something."

"Hey guys, this is a good spot." Carmen walks up.

"Did you buy something?"

She shakes her head and scrunches up her nose. "No, I ended up not buying anything. They don't have original Micheladas. They're kinda expensive here anyway."

"We should come here during happy hour." Trent looks up from his hammock.

"Sure, one day."

I try to relax, but something about that sign we saw earlier keeps bothering me.

"Hey guys, you all saw that black and white poster outside on the curb, right?"

Alice gasps. "Yeah, you mean the one that says, enjoy the collaps—"

"Yeah, that one!"

"Right."

"I don't know what they're doing, but I know ICE is involved." Carmen gets up to attention.

"You mean U.S. Immigration and Customs Enforcement." Trent gazes at me while swinging in his hammock.

"Yeah, we're all gonna get sent back to Mexico." Carmen mocks and rocks on the hammock, rolling her dark eyes.

"God, I remember when I used to work at Pei Wei. When I first started working there, all the cooks were Mexican. And they were the best cooks on the line, even though they barely spoke any English."

"Mmmmhmm." Carmen nods.

"At the time, the manager didn't care. Partly because they were the best cooks he ever had. So, one day after President Trump was elected. Someone from P.F. Chang's company came in and found out they were all illegal immigrants and fired all of them at once." — I snap my fingers. "Just like that."

"Oh wow."

"And then—"

"Maybe that's why I can't get a decent Michelada here anymore." Carmen interrupts me.

I laugh. "Anyway, and then, the next day, there's a lunch rush, and the only people on the wok line are these two white guys. One of them was just hired and can't even toss a wok for shit."

Carmen interjects again. "—Are you telling me... A shrimp fried this rice?"

I giggle as I am trying to finish my story. "So, as a result, everyone's food is backed up, and people are waiting for their food for at least 40 minutes. This one woman yells at me that she's been waiting longer than other people who just got their food and just chews me out before leaving, saying that she's going to miss her flight because of the wait."

"Jesus." Ron shakes his head.

"I know, right? She actually gave me the dirtiest looks. Other people were so mad, and some of them, when they finally got their food, said it was runny and tasted terrible. So they all went up and asked for a refund."

"After it was all over, I went in the back and cried. It was the worst day at work ever; I thought about quitting that day."

"Wow, I would've." Carmen looks down.

"Well, you've seen what's been happening with the Mexican immigrants coming in en masse, who are being sent by Mexican officials in response to Trump's wall. After he claimed (Ron makes air quotes) that Mexico's going to pay for it." Ron discusses this with the group.

Carmen nods. "Yeah, Trump said that they're sending in rapists and drug runners into the U.S. saying we all have herpes. And some people actually agree with him."

"You mean the rednecks?" Trent scoffs.

"Trump is spreading hate and distrust among the people who live on the southern border, among the Mexican community. When in reality, he needs us."—

"Right." I agree.

"He needs the undocumented people to work for him for cheap labor." Carmen talks with her hands.

"Based," Trent adds.

Ron speaks up. "Apparently, they've put so many illegal immigrants in ICE camps they've started putting them in county jails. And the jails... they get paid by ICE for detaining immigrants."

"It's getting really bad. So many Mexican children have been separated from their parents..."

I slump back in my hammock. "Ugh, I can't believe we're stuck with him. I feel oppressed."

"It's not just him." Carmen puts down her phone. "It's the entire U.S. government and the capitalists."

"But mostly the Capitalists, the Bankers, the Economists," Ron added.

"Ohhhh, hot shit," I said.

Carmen has since expressed her regard for Trump, that voting for him was the lesser of the two evils. I can't remember if she voted or not. I didn't vote; I don't vote for Presidential figures.

"Don't even get me started. Right now, the senate is trying to impeach President Trump."

"Good luck with that." I huff.

Ron sits forward in his hammock. "I mean seriously, they take a hunk of our money in taxes, leaving us poor. Meanwhile, they use that tax money to pay ICE, who is making money by separating these families, and they're forcing these kids into the foster system or worse. Selling these kids off to human traffickers."

"Yeah, people are protesting this." Carmen raises her eyebrows and rocks herself in the hammock.

"Let's eat the rich," Trent's voice booms.

"Yeah, let's," I reply, figuratively, of course.

Trent gets up and finds a seat on a metal lawn chair. "Everyone is saying that Gen Z and millennials are canceling all these subpar franchises when, in actuality, it's because we can't afford the same moronic bullshit that boomers could afford."

Carmen laughs lightheartedly.

"Valid," Ron glances and makes a finger gun at Trent in approval.

"F***ing... back in my day..." Trent imitates an old man's raspy voice.

"I was working for $6.00 an hour as a paper boy." He gets up, hunches over, holds his back, and sucks on his lips like he's wearing a pair of dentures. Carmen and I snicker at his impression.

"And... and I was able to afford my two-story home in Indiana. And 7 years later," he sucks on his teeth, "I bought my lake house in Vermont..." Trent goes over to Ron and nudges his hammock. "See, boy..." Trent taps his forehead. "That's where hard work gets ya...."

Ron smiles his gambler's grin. "Sure thing, Grandpa." He plays along with his charade.

I look at Trent and take the conversation seriously. "Yeah, when both of those homes cost like $26,000 back then. Literally pocket change compared to what those homes cost now."

Carmen sits up and reads from her phone. "...I just looked up the inflation rate, and it turns out $6.00 per hour in 1980 has the same buying power as $20.00 per hour in 2020."

"Jesus," Ron utters from his spot. "Where does all that money go? Minimum wage isn't keeping up with inflation."

I look up at Ron, "I know, right? Minimum wage right now is still $7.25 per hour." I stop, thinking about how I'm still only getting paid $9.50 as a bagger. Damn.

"Eat the f***ing richhhhhhh!!!" Trent growls through his teeth.

Carmen joins in, in a nasal voice, "Uhhh... why do you still live in your mom's attic?" Like she was imitating one of her frenemies. "Because I can't afford to live anywhere!"

"Haha, nooooooo!" I feel her plight; I'm still stuck at home at 21.

Carmen continues, now talking with her hands. "And now I have my mom asking me when I am going to give her grandchildren. Like she didn't just ask me to pay for rent for my own room." We all felt that. "Shit, I know, right." Ron lays back again.

"Mmmm, I felt that..." Trent breathes in his menthol vape. "...That we aren't having enough children. We can't even afford to take care of ourselves or buy a house. So f*** rich people's Pier 1, we can't afford expensive, cheaply made furniture for our non-existing house. F*** Toys R ass," everyone roars with laughter. "No one can afford to have kids; we definitely aren't buying toys for non-existing kids."

I stop laughing. I remember reading how Amazon and other stores sold toys for a lot cheaper than Toys R Us and how a lot of kids are more into digital toys now.

Ron's laughter dies, and he takes a hit from his vape. "Heck, having kids. I'm just trying to live."

"I don't even want to have kids," Carmen gets off her phone and looks up at the sky.

***

Carmen's cat, Merida, finally gave birth at 4:24 am last night. Merida gave birth to two kittens, one black and one gray like her. The last one, the gray kitten, wasn't breathing. We tried rubbing it to see if it would breathe but to no avail… The gray one was stillborn. With Carmen's permission, we buried him in the backyard. Merida already gave birth twice, but she was still huddled in her box and panting like she had more kittens in her. She's so stressed she won't let her newborn kitten feed. The mama Cat's gotta eat too.

I open my phone to text Carmen.

Me: She's being really protective right now. And growling.

Carmen: That's okay. Awww, those motherly instincts. Okie.

I lift up the blue flowery sheet to watch her.

Me: Barely, Ron's gonna pick you up. She's falling asleep now.

Merida curls up with her head down and slows her breathing down. Sweet kitty, she's so tired from her first labor.

Carmen: Yeah, I named her Sol because Luna-moon Sol-sun.

I look at her lone black kitten as it's squirming around.

Me: What about Sunni?

Carmen: Nah.

Me: Name her Uno because she's the first one.

I look at the small, defenseless kitten. (And maybe the only one.)

Carmen: Eh.

I look up what to do with newborn kittens on my Android.

"Newborn kittens are born blind (they open their eyes at anywhere from seven to fourteen days after birth) and, therefore, must be kept safe and warm at all times." I grab a gray Spider-Man fleece blanket that Carmen left and place it over the squirmy kitten.

A knock at the door alerts me that Ron is back with Carmen and Trent. They open the door and stand in the doorway.

"Hey guys, she's doing well, but she's still tightening like there's more babies in her."

"Don't touch her! Or the kitten, your smell could make her reject her baby," Carmen warns me.

"It's fine. She's not a wild animal," Trent dismisses her. His major should've been a veterinarian before the drugs messed him up in high school.

"I don't know... I just need the baby to be healthy."

We end up spending the rest of the afternoon at Carmen's house waiting for Merida to give her the last kitten.

We all gather in a half-circle around the TV. Trent and Ron are set on watching the new movie Parasite. It's a Korean drama about a poor family who tricks a rich family into hiring them to do housework.

Ten minutes into the movie, Merida starts to lighten and pant.

"Oh, Merida, you okay?" I ask the cat.

She meows like she's in pain.

"Ohhhh my baby." Carmen crouches over Merida's box.

Merida pants and looks up at her owner. The black kitten finishes suckling.

"I think we should take her to the vet," Carmen says in a worried tone.

"We could take her to the one in Kingwood, The Kings crossing animal hospital," I suggest to her.

"No, we aren't taking her there. Anywhere in Kingwood is too expensive," Carmen says from the bathroom as she grabs Merida's carrier. Merida folds her ears back and howls as soon as she sees Carmen come in with the plastic crate carrier.

"Come on, Merida, it's okay." Carmen's black hair falls in her face as she bends over to coax the cat.

Merida hisses at her but slowly calms down as Carmen gently picks her up and places her and her kitten in the carrier.

"Ron, can you look up cheap emergency animal care centers?" Carmen asks as she closes the small metal gate on Merida's carrier.

"Yeah, one sec." Ron looks at his Android.

"There's one by the mall."

"Okay, let's take her there."

Merida starts to meow in distress from her carrier on the ground next to the front door.

"Awwww, Poor baby," Carmen says as she gets ready at the bathroom vanity.

"Where are we taking her?" I ask Ron.

"The Emergency animal care center by the Deerbrook mall."

I know which one he's talking about.

"Oh, yeah." I look at his phone. "I took my dog, Skye; thereafter, she was bitten by a copperhead snake on my birthday."

"Awww, was Skye okay?" Carmen asks.

"Poor Skye," Ron replies.

"Tragic," Trent deadpans.

"Yeah, the vet says she was recovering on her own. Something about her blood started to coagulate, but they gave her an antivenom and some steroids."

"Oh, okay, as long as she's okay." Carmen finishes up her makeup.

"Yeah, you know Skye's not dead." I get up to stretch and get ready to leave.

We take Carmen's car to the 24-hour Emergency veterinary care center. It's an outdated building to the right of the Deerbrook Mall parking lot. We carry Merida in her carrier inside.

Carmen checks in at the front desk on the right as she briefly describes the problem to the lady at the counter. While me and the boys, Trent and Ron, take our seats in the dark gray waiting area. I look up to see a TV overhead playing reruns of the TV series Friends.

A few other people are waiting here, too, a dad and his daughter with a drooling brown bloodhound on a leash. And a quiet elderly couple.

We sit and wait in the waiting room for a while. Trent reclines and lifts up his legs to cross them. His bright neon yellow lace-up Nike brand shoes prop up with him.

"I like your shoes," the elderly woman compliments Trent's shoes, but he doesn't notice.

"Trent! Trent." I call out to him.

"Young man..." The elderly woman interjects.

"Hmm?" He looks toward me and the old woman. "I like your shoes; they're very nice." She leans forward.

"Oh, thank you." Trent nods and smiles a rare smile.

"I'd like a pair like those," she says, almost in a whisper.

After 43 minutes of the TV show Friends reruns, the gray door behind the counter swings open, and Carmen comes out with Merida.

"So everything's okay; the vet says she's experiencing a phantom birth. The vet checked to see if she had any more babies in her, and she doesn't."

"Well, that's... that's good, at least," Ron says, confused about what a phantom birth is.

"How much did the vet charge?"

"Not that much, just like $60 dollars."

"Here, take Merida. I'll drive us." She hands me the carrier. The green plastic crate. I peer into it, and Merida looks at me with wild eyes, still exhausted from birth but not allowed to sleep.

I place Merida on my lap as we drive. She shuffles around for a while until she finds a comfortable position. When we get back to Carmen's house, I bring the crate into her room and let the cat out along with her kitten. Everyone settles in to watch the movie Parasite. Once we start the movie, we aren't even ten minutes in until Carmen stops the movie again.

"Guys, I am kinda hungry."

"Okay," I chuckle. "I wanna get to the end of this movie eventually."

We throw around ideas of going to McDonald's or Taco Bell since it's close, and it's what we usually get when we're drunk. We finally give up on trying to decide and just leave. Carmen stays behind to watch over Merida.

"I don't really feel like driving. I'm too tired from waking up early. Can you drive, Ron?"

"Yeah, sure." I hand him my keys.

Ron drives around to the back of Kingwood to the middle of Town Center. We drive through the road inside a grove of oak trees.

"Where are we going?" I ask him.

"You'll see."

"Feels like I'm going crazy."

"Well, looks like you're already there." He looks at me through the dashboard mirror.

"Shut up." I smile at him.

The car finally makes a stop at the Whataburger drive-thru. A Texas favorite: Whataburger. It's a burger place where they serve you real meat in a large burger. It isn't a choice; all their burgers are that big. It's so huge, it's almost bigger than your hand. They even have Dr. Pepper shakes. Who else does that? And if you're on a diet, they have salads with whole slices of real bacon in them. It's no surprise every time I look at our local Whataburger, there is always a line in the drive-thru, even after 12 am.

I open up my phone.

Me: Hey, what do you want from Whataburger?

Carmen: French fries are the only thing I can eat, lol.

We order, the boys get burgers, and I try the new buffalo chicken sandwich. We make it back to Carmen's house with our Whataburger sustenance in hand and have a Whataburger feast on Carmen's carpet floor as we start up the movie Parasite, a highly-rated movie.

Once the movie is over, I look at Carmen to see her reaction.

"Oh wow, that ending was great. The whole time, the rock was— wow."

"Yeah, I know. The plot was great, really original."

Trent lets out a muted burp, "Yeah, it really showed the social and economic inequality between the poor and the wealthy class in South Korea."

"True, the poor family deserved better..."

"Hah, okay, hot take." I laugh.

Carmen cleans up the burger wrappers and puts them in the paper bags.

"So, if we go to Vegas for Valentine's, we need to buy cheap flights now. We can use my Hilton discount at Hilton hotels." Carmen tells everyone while she lays on her stomach, scrolling on her phone.

Ron looks at her incredulously. "We can't go to Vegas, Carmen. I can't afford flights to Nevada." Ron shakes his shaggy hair.

"Can't you just get your parents to pay for your flights?"

"No, Carmen, my parents aren't rich."

"Carmen, he can't go to Vegas." Trent reads the room.

"Ugh! You guys are such losers, but I really want to goooo!"

"Well, it's not gonna happen. I'm not going to Las Vegas." Ron tells her.

"This isn't just about you, Ron. It's about all of us having a vote about where to go, Adri—do you want to go to Vegas?"

I look away from her to the floor. "Uhhhh... Carmen, I'm not really into gambling."

"See, Adri doesn't want to go on your irresponsible plan to go to Las Vegas." He stares at Carmen begrudgingly.

"Shut up, Ron. You don't have to gamble, Adri. If you go, there's other things to do there." She huffs. Carmen turns to Trent. "What about you, Trent?"

"I'll go with you."

"Yeah? Seriously?"

"I'd be down."

They start to talk to each other in low voices on her bed on the floor.

"I've never been to San Antonio. Not without my parents anyway." Ron tells us.

"You wanna go... to the Alamo?" I ask him.

"Yea—NO, we are not going to San Antonio." Carmen snaps at him.

"Why not?" Ron asks.

"There is nothing to do there; it's just the Alamo and the River Walk, and that's it. Why don't we just go to Austin for the Valentine's weekend?" I suggest.

"I go to Austin all the time. I used to live there, remember?" She says, groaning.

I speak up. "I've never been to Austin on my own."

"You've never been to 6th Street?" She looks at me in shock.

"No, but I might have driven past it on my way to my sister's soccer tournament."

"At night?" She sits up.

"Nope." I stare wide-eyed.

"When you go, all the bars and nightclubs are open, and the streets are packed, and everyone is out walking and being gay, and there's vendors on the street."

"Uh-huh." Trent nods with a smile.

"It's like a fair every weekend night."

Carmen looks toward Trent. "Remember that one time we went on 6th Street and met that gorgeous drag queen that bought us all shots?"

"Mmm hmmm yeah, that was fun. She was hot and dangerous." Trent's expression turns into a sly smile.

10

The Trip

But I need Trent, A.K.A. Triston B., to write this page. I need his help to write this page as a chance to redeem himself.

He goes by Gulag on Discord, and he's tagged on my Instagram page. They gotta be here somewhere.

I look all around my messy room for the earrings I just bought at the mall. "Ugh, where the f*** are they!" I yell to myself.

I go into my closet to search my vintage jewelry box. I toss aside black bat earrings from last year's Halloween party that I only wore once. Not here.

I look into my old shopping bags, but they're empty. Until I see something glistening behind my keyboard on my desk. I grab them. There they are; my heart-shaped earrings bordered by pearls and diamonds. I pack them into a small silk bag for the trip.

My parents and my sister finish up eating dinner, but I decline. I am still full of poetry pizza and a really good feeling. My poem made people feel like they could feel a sense of longing. A longing I feel all the time. A longing for acceptance. A yearning to find myself inside my poetry.

Ever since I started college, I've felt uneasy and distressed. My soul can't remember true peace. That's why I create it through prose. A small piece for myself, a piece of Island tranquility just for me. A place where I can escape to and leave my haunted past behind. Hopefully, this too shall pass, and I'll graduate soon.

My phone lights up.

I open the notification. It's Carmen.

Carmen: Hey, hop on Discord.

Me: Okay.

I close my messages and go to my Discord app.

> *Carmadlg added Adri29 to the group*

Gulag: Uhm, hello Adri29.

I guess Trent is Gulag.

Carmadlg: 7712 E. Riverside Drive, Austin TX 78744 US Phone: 15123891616 Check-in Fri. Feb 14. 2 nights, Checkout 12:00 pm Sat. Feb 15.

I save the screenshot of the hotel information to my phone. With our trip to Austin, it'll be a good chance to forget my trauma and have a good time with my friends. With no parental supervision. I repeat, NO PARENTAL SUPERVISION, and all the alcohol we can afford at the quirky yet fashionable bars on Austin's 6th street.

I open my phone to see what the gang is up to before I go into work at 4.

Me: What are ya'll doing today?

Gulag: eat> nut> sleep

Me: Oh?

Carmadlg: The big three, Classic.

Gulag: Ye.

I laugh at Trent. To be honest, that's probably what he's actually doing.

Me: Heyyyyy, Ya'll wanna stop by Buc-ees on the way to Austin?

Flux: Of course. I can't survive without my beaver nuggets.

(Flux is Ron's Discord name.)

Me: Lmaooo, those things are nastyyy.

Flux: SO GROSS.

Me: I'll make some popcorn and sweets for the trip.

Flux: Okay, bet.

I'm starting to see why Carmen thinks Ron always goes with what I say. Which... might not be a bad thing. I like it when I get my way with my man; I realize that now. As long as he's intelligent. I could never date a stupid man. I like what I've got with Ron; he's intuitive but not too pretentious either, a humble man.

I check the clock; it's almost 3:50. I live only six minutes away from my job. Which is convenient, I guess. All the high-paying jobs are mostly in the city. If I want to find a starter graphic design job in Houston, then the distance would be farther. I would end up paying half of what I make just to get to work. Ugh. My only chance of making money in design would be to find a work-from-home job that will even hire a beginner.

I get to work and clock in at 4:00 and daydream about my Star Wars project. While I bag strangers' groceries, I picture myself as a Jedi in training. I imagine myself clashing lightsabers against droids to Guns N' Roses. It would be so cool to use the Force in real life. Or have mind powers and a way to defend myself against the forces of evil, or just a way to walk alone safely at night. A lightsaber in my left hand and the power to use the Force in my right.

"Hey, can you put this lunch meat back?" The cashier holds up a Boar's Head brand ham in front of my hands. "The customer didn't want it."

I sigh as the cashier interrupts my thoughts and grab the meat begrudgingly. After work is over at 10 pm, I check the Discord chat.

Carmadlg: Bitch guess who's getting a raise.

Gulag: Not you.

Flux: Me.

Carmadlg: Nvm then damn.

Flux: Bitch who.

Carmadlg: Me, bitch tf.

Flux: How much?

Gulag: Good job, bro.

Carmadlg: Idek yet, but they're doing my three-month review and they're considering me for management in the future.

Flux: Very f***ing cool. Good job, dude.

Gulag: Agreed. Extremely based.

Carmadlg: Thank u :)

ALSO My job is hiring. Just letting ya'll know.

Gulag: Gib job lol.

Flux: Oh shit, might have to slide in.

Gulag: To do what though?

Carmadlg: Yeah, they never hire, but someone is leaving for maternity leave and someone got another job at the same time so, front desk and kitchen. Kitchen is easy af.

Flux: I WILL WORK KITCHEN.

Carmadlg: You work by yourself and it's either 5 am-1 pm or 3 pm-9 pm.

Flux: Not bad at all.

Carmadlg: The nights are only Mon-Thurs too.

Flux: Bruh, I lost 20 pounds. Idk how that happened. I weighed like 220; I'm down to 199.

Gulag: Cool.

Carmadlg: That's awesome.

Flux: Ty ty.

Carmadlg: They're having project grad here. For KPARK high school.

Flux: LOL WTF.

Gulag: Bruh.

Flux: Wtf are they gonna do.

Carmadlg: Idek.

Flux: Not sleep.

Gulag: F***.

Flux: Precisely.

Gulag: I have laundry to do and there's no water at my house.

Carmadlg: Sooo what time tomorrow?? Oh shit, that sucks. Do you wanna do some at my place tonight or something?

Gulag: My parents are using my sister's place. I should be able to get ready there tonight lol. If not, I'll let you know.

Carmadlg: Oof okay lol.

Carmadlg: Is Adri at work?

Flux: I think so yeah. Hmmm, there might be a problem with picking up Trent tomorrow.

Suddenly, it dawns on me. "Oh, shit!" I forgot that my project for After Effects is due this weekend. I slap my hands on my face and drag the tips of my fingers into my cheeks. I won't have a chance to finish it up this weekend because of the trip.

I run downstairs and plop down in front of the computer and open up my save file on After Effects. "Ughhhhhhhh..." I groan. It's going to be a long night.

I've already created a garbage bag or whatever my professor calls it; a mask over the video of my body swinging around a toy lightsaber in front of a massive green screen.

My professor sent us links to videos on YouTube for lightsaber tutorials. I watch the whole video and go back to it for reference while I work.

Everyone's asleep while I toil away at my computer. I look at the clock; it's 2:30 am. I turn around in the dimly lit living room to watch my dogs sleep. My oldest dog, Teddy, twitches his leg as he dreams. I wonder what his little dog mind is dreaming of. He whisper barks in his sleep and twitches again. He's probably dreaming of running around in the woods, chasing squirrels with Skye. I wish I could be like him, sound asleep.

I turn around and, grasp my mouse and get to work on fixing the shadow levels so that the video of me matches the shadows and highlights of the Star Wars space palace. I fix the saturation as well, making myself more golden and adding a green beam of light to my lightsaber. I double back a few times after I play the video to fix some mistakes.

I look through my blue light protection glasses for beams of lasers in the special effects tabs, but to no avail. I look back to the college website to find any downloads; sure enough, I find a red shooting beam effect to add.

I manipulate the red beams to disappear when my saber hits them. I start to feel like a real special effects movie editor.

When it's all complete, I look at the clock: 4:28 am. Damn, I spent all night finishing my Star Wars edit. I compress my video and save it into my sacred white geometric USB. If I lost this baby, I would lose almost all of my completed graphic effects projects.

I lean back into my chair and stretch my arms out. I let out a yawn so loud I almost wake my parents. OK, my class starts at 9 am. I saunter upstairs to my bed for a three-hour nap. I wake up to my phone's alarm and wash my heavy eyes. My heart pangs and pains my chest, unused to waking up like this. I am still sluggish, so I try to fix it by downing a cup of burnt coffee.

I load up all my luggage into my white Hyundai, my first car. So that when I finish class, I'll head straight to

Carmen's. She's the closest from the college. Then I'll go to Ron's and finally Trent's.

I drive to class past the divides of towering trees and bushes, past the clearing with local businesses. I'm anticipating the drive to Austin; I rub the crust that I missed from the corner of my eye. After I break through the surge of early traffic, I drive underneath the main highway to get to Lone Star College. I drive to my usual parking lot, but all the spaces are full, so I end up parking on the side of the road closest to my class. Other cars are parked on the stretch of curb by the man-made pond, so I know it's okay.

I toss on my army green backpack and trod through the fresh dew grass to my After Effects class.

I reach the sidewalks that lead up to the tan brick building. The college is enclosed in a pine tree forest with a man-made pond bordering the college. I walk past the small courtyard surrounding a birdbath and through the glass doors to my computer class.

I arrive there earlier than I usually do. Other students are making their way inside as well.

I send a text on the Discord chat at 8:30.

Me: Hey, I'm picking ya'll up at around 10.

Carmadlg: Trent won't be done till later; we're gonna have to leave at noon ish.

Me: Wut what's Trent doing???

Carmadlg: Yeah, he has no water at his house so he has to go do laundry. It's okay, we'll make it right after check-in time.

Flux: Bet I'm taking a longer nap.

Carmadlg: Be ready by 11:30-11:45.

Flux: Will do.

"Good morning, everyone," my professor strides in. "I'll wait until everyone comes in. Those of you who are already here, open up After Effects and Illustrator."

Adobe Illustrator and After Effects tabs pop up on the overhead projector. Once the class is full, the professor begins the lesson.

"As you all know, your homework is to turn in the Star Wars lightsaber edit into the Turnitin folder on the class website this weekend." He moves his mouse to the college website. "I see some of you have already turned it in."

That was me. I've never worked so fast overnight. It's actually rare for me to turn projects in early. I'm known to procrastinate on projects I don't have interest in, but this last one was really fun.

Our professor then pulls up a video. He clicks on a thumbnail from our class's website. It's a video of a film student holding out his hands in a field as a circle of runes and symbols that glow and sparkle appear and rotate around his controlled hand motions, just like the magic Doctor Strange uses in the Avenger movies.

After the clip is over, our professor makes everyone come up and shoot videos on an HD Canon Camera (the kind he lends out to the students for projects). No one wants to get up and look like an idiot, so the professor starts calling up random students to take videos of us moving our hands around like we were monks training in the Doctor Strange movie.

I was not dressed to make this video. I'd look like a total rookie magic user with my red plaid button-up and denim jeans. I'm called up, and I assume the position everyone else was doing with my twist. The professor makes me do it again after claiming it wasn't at the right angle.

The professor finishes filming and looks up from his camera setup.

I look at the clock. Damn, it's already 11:25! It took us 2 hours just to film everyone waving and flailing in the air.

"Alright, I will be... posting everyone's video on the school website this weekend." He gets up and moves to his desk in the corner by the projector screen. "The next step is to create the swirling symbols or... what is it?"

"...Runes?" a student calls out.

"Runes?" So this is what the Millennials are into?

"Yeah."

"Okay, we're gonna animate a rotating wheel of magic runes in After Effects."

Whispers of the Avenger movies murmur through the room.

"Yes, just like in Doctor Strange..." He clumsily moves his rotund body around his desktop, clicks his mouse, pulls up a reflecting format in Illustrator, creates a twelfth-of-a-circle design, and watches it repeat itself into a full circle.

"Another way we can do this is by creating two circles, one smaller than the other, and then writing some random words in Wingdings font. Or some other alien language." The classroom stifles a chuckle.

"And make sure to write it on a curved line in between the two circles to make a 'rune' floating thing or whatever." He drones. I feel like he's been doing the same lesson for years and became endlessly bored with the monotony of teaching the same lessons every year. Like his heart isn't in it anymore, just his paycheck.

I follow his instructions and make my own magic circle.

"Now, we create the geometric diamond and squares to go in the middle."

I copy the professor's instructions. I even go out on my own and do some intricate designs in the pentagrams.

I get a notification on my phone from Discord.

Gulag: My clothes need one more speed cycle in the dryer; my water's back on, so I'm back home to shower, etc. So like 30-40 min and I'll be good, I think.

Flux: Big bet.

Me: Yee

Carmadlg: Traffic is going to be awful. Even just getting around Kingwood rn is badddd.

I turn my phone over and resume his instructions. I decide my runes are gonna glow purple, so I add in the preset to make the spinning pentagrams glow purple and time the spinning effects just right. It looks authentic enough to me, like if I am learning Doctor. Strange magic in a different dimension. I look at the clock. It's already 12:05.

I open the chat.

Me: Someone call me so I have an excuse to bounce from class.

I look around the room anticipating the call.

Ron makes my phone buzz, a few people look at the disturbance.

I look at my phone.

"If it's an emergency, please leave." The professor sighs.

"Sorry, 'scuse me." I exit the computer room and answer his call.

"Hello?" I put my phone next to my ear.

"Hey," it's Carmen on the line. "I'm ready; I already picked up Ron so you don't have to stop at his place."

"Okay, sounds good."

"Everything okay?" She asks.

"Yeah, everything's fine; I'm in class right now. But I don't know if I can drive all the way to Austin. I had to stay up all night to finish my stupid Star Wars project."

"Adri... We literally made plans for this trip. I already booked the hotel—an"

"It's fine." I cut her off before she took my head off. "It's fine; I can just get Ron to drive us there. He can drive. Plus, he just had a nap."

"Ugh, fine. If you can get him to drive anyway."

"It'll be fine."

"Okay, just come and pick us up."

"Okay, I'm on my way."

She hangs up.

I come back into the early 2000s furnished classroom to pick up my stuff and shut down my computer.

The professor is mentoring one of the students at their computer when I leave. No one even bats an eye.

That's just how college is.

You're an adult now and treated as such. You're free to make your own decisions in college, not like high school. Everyone has somewhere to be; most of them have jobs to go to secret double lives outside of campus. They don't offer room and board here, so people have to drive their cars or ride with friends to get to class. Some students are even parents and have to worry about their own children. I've even seen middle-aged and elderly people take classes to get better jobs and promotions. In some ways, I'm relieved, relieved that if I ever change majors one day, it will be normal, and I won't be seen as a failure. It just goes to show how it's never too late to start over or start again.

I exit the building; the sun is brighter and higher in the sky now. I yawn as I pad through the crabgrass. My eyelids are getting heavier now. Shit...

I drive to Carmen's house with dreary eyes. I arrive at her home and honk my horn. They're probably sitting on her burlap couch waiting for me.

Carmen and Ron come out with bags in hand, Carmen with two bags and Ron with one giant duffel bag. I help them arrange their luggage into my trunk. Ron lifts his bag with a grunt. It looks heavy.

"What do you have in there? A dead body?"

"Nope, just my shit."

"Damn, dude, if it's just your shit, maybe think about eating more fiber?"

"Uh, gross..." Carmen groans, but I can see her smile.

I look at the trunk; I put my hand on the lifted trunk door.

"...So...is that it? Everybody got everything?" I ask.

"Yeah," Carmen and Ron take a moment to look around.

"Y'all didn't forget anything, right? Chargers? Toothbrush?" They stand outside in the driveway; Ron pats his pants pocket. His hand moves up to his red plaid shirt pockets.

"Oh wait, I forgot something." Carmen hustles hurriedly back to her Phthalo green house.

Ron steps around the car towards the Navigator's door.

"Wait!" I stand in front of him before he can open the door.

"What's up?" He asks.

"Can I ask you a favor?" Now I am asking.

"Okay, what's that?" He folds his arms, expecting something difficult.

"Do you think you can..." I look down at my feet shuffling on the concrete.

"Can you drive us to Austin?"

"Seriously, Adri?" He sighs.

"Yes, I had to stay up all night to finish my project for college last night and I didn't get any sleep." I toss my arms up. "I'll fall asleep at the wheel if I drive." I beg him with my eyes and my lower lip stuck out.

"Fine, I guess I'll drive." He relents. "But you owe me." He unfolds his red plaid arms.

"Yes, my king." I smile, and fake bow to him in relief.

"That's right." He enters the driver's side of my white Hyundai and buckles himself up. "And you're my queen."

He looks at me and leans in to kiss me, and I meet him and close the gap between our lips.

Carmen comes back with a pair of pink flip-flops, and then tosses them in my trunk.

She slides into the back seat, and sees us looking at her. " I need them just in case; I've worked in hotels before and you never know who uses hotel showers."

"True, places can be really nasty." Ron turns around to look back at the driveway to back out.

"Alright, let's go pick up that bum. Hopefully, he got his clothes washed by now."

"I'm on it." Ron backs out into the street, well, it's more like a black asphalt road.

"Oh, so you asked Ron to drive? Are you sure you're good enough to drive three hours?"

"Yeah, I can drive; I already have my license." We accelerate to 30mph round the bend of the road next to a white gazebo claimed by nature. I close my eyes for a bit, relieved that Ron can drive us there. It's nice to let someone else take the wheel for a while.

I regain consciousness when I start to feel the car slow down and drive up a slope. Opening my eyes, I find Trent coming out of his house. Ron crouches down to open the lever that opens the trunk. The back trunk opens up and lets Trent pack his stuff in.

"Hey, Trent."

"Happy Valentine's Day!"

"What's up?" Trent opens the passenger door and slides in.

"Ready to go?"

"Yeah, finally, I almost had to go to the dry cleaners."

"Good thing too." Ron starts the car. "Now we don't have to smell your ass all the way there."

Trent kicks the back of Ron's seat. The car jolts forward a foot.

"Hey! I'm driving, Trent. I go down, we all go down."

"Trent, stop kicking his seat." Carmen warns.

"Did you hear what he said to me?"

Ron adjusts his steering and turns the car around, back to the main road.

So, this is it, The Journey Begins...

"Guys, I am actually really hungry. Can we stop somewhere?" I hear Carmen's output from the backseat.

"Okay, where should we stop?" The car hitches up as we drive up over the hills with tunnels underneath, surrounded by forests.

"I wanted to try the Impossible Whopper at Burger King."

They have this new promotion going on at Burger King called the Impossible Whopper. The burger is supposed to be a vegan patty that tastes exactly like the original Whopper.

Carmen recently decided to become a vegan again. She claimed it helped her lose weight. I could never become Vegan, ever. Meat is protein and your body needs protein to maintain a healthy balance. Besides that, shrimp and steak are so delicious. I can't forget about Texas Barbecue either; It's a Texas staple.

We cruise through the groves of elm trees to Kingwood's town center. It looks like a little block of Manhattan in Texas. Or at least that's what they tell me. We stop at Burger King's drive-through. Carmen orders her Impossible Whopper; Trent orders chicken tenders, and I share a large drink and large fries with Ron.

I nibble on the thick-cut fries. I hate being tired and hungry at the same time, especially when I sleep after eating.

Carmen and Trenton gain control of the aux cord.

I turn my head towards the backseat. "Hey guys, I made a road trip playlist."

Carmen doesn't look up from her phone. "We can listen to it later; me and Trent want to listen to Deftones right now."

I remember watching an interview about the band Deftones; the lead singer, Chino Moreno, wanted to create metal music that was also offset by deep emotional vocals. That he wanted to make music you could really bump and grind to.

We make it out of the fortress of forests that is Kingwood and head southwest towards Houston. I look out at the car as we get on the highway. *Be quiet and drive (far away)* by Deftones starts to play.

"This town doesn't feel mine."

The car sways back and forth through cars and overpasses on highway 69. I could hear the whimpers and the whispers embedded between hard bass lines in the song, *Be quiet and drive (far away),* and it made me want to. *"I'm fast to get away, far."*

I space out between the rhythm and the melodies. It makes me think of sex, definitely car sex.

"I dressed you in her clothes."

"Now drive me far away, away, away."

I lean back and dive into the music. I deeply listen to the lyrics, thinking about how every man has a warm, tender, emotional side, just as women have a logical, rational knowing side. I just want to know if my hidden parts will meld with Ron's secret parts so we may both be happy in our relationship. But how? How will I know if our love is enough? If it is love, and not just lust.

"It feels good to know you're mine."

I'm just now finding out about how he is, as much as how I am finding out about myself, and how I am, in this bond. Some deep subconscious part of me already knows how I truly feel about Ron.

"Now drive me far away, away, away."

I look out at the hot, grassy landscape littered with unfinished construction and broken billboards as we leave Houston city limits.

"Hey Adriana, I thought you were gonna make popcorn?"

"Oh, Fuuuuck. I forgot." I open the car compartments under the tortoise shell dashboard trim, expecting the popcorn to magically appear in the car that way.

"It's fine; we can stop at Buc-ees," Carmen interjects.

A few more miles down the stretch of plains, and we see a sign for Buc-ee's exit within 5 miles, the cheeky little beaver beckoning us to come into Buc-ee's.

Ah, Buc-ee's – a glorified gas station and rest stop. All my best road trips begin and end with Buc-ees. Just seeing a Buc-ee's billboard after a 5-hour trip across the coastal plains made my younger self scream and beg for my parents to stop the car at Beaverland. Of course, you can't miss it – with giant billboards in the middle of nowhere that say "Eat here. Get gas" or "My overbite is sexy" with the giant cheeky beaver logo. Or another (my dad's favorite) "Risk it for the brisket" which he has been saying for the last 15 years.

We come off the main road and take the exit towards Buc-ee's. A bronze Buc-ee's beaver statue greets us at the entrance. Once we walk inside, it's packed full of people from all over Texas. Some are dressed in pajamas and look like they just woke up. Both sides of the store entrance are lined with cashier stands. My nose is filled with the delicious smell of BBQ. I look, and I see the heart of the store, a sign catches my eye that says "Texas Round up" underneath which is the food being prepped by line cooks. They hand out in-house made kettle-cooked chips and of course create the famous slow-cooked-barbecued-brisket. Alongside is pulled-pork, turkey, sausage, and all of the above you can have in a sandwich or wrap. In the middle, refrigerated stands with grab-and-go meals like salads, cheese and meat samplers, cut fruit, or veggies. They even have key-lime pie in a cup. Towards the back left side, they have in-house made fudge and sugar-covered-roasted nuts that you can smell throughout the store.

I look around me to see if my friends are around, but they are already out hounding for food. I grab a brisket sandwich and make my way towards the regular gas station stocked items to the assorted fountain drink station. They have so many different flavors, some I have never even seen before. I grab a medium Styrofoam cup, fill up on Arizona tea (my favorite drink), and make my way past the swaths of people towards the exit.

I count heads as I wait in the car. Everyone is here except Trent.

"Where's Trent?" I look back at Carmen.

"Oh, he's still waiting on his food," she says through bites of her spicy wrap.

A few minutes later, Trent appears through the glass doors with his hand carrying a Buc-ee's plastic bag and the other in his pocket.

Trent tucks into the car and pulls out a Styrofoam container from the bag.

"What did you get?" Carmen asks, staring at his food.

"Pulled pork sandwich and fries." He opens the lid and shoves the sandwich in his face.

"Finally, let's get going." Ron starts up the car and cruises onto the highway to continue the journey to Austin.

I finish my savory brisket sandwich and fall asleep to the sway and motion of the car ride.

"Oh, wowww... Look!" I wake up to the sound of Carmen's wonder as she points out to the window. I rub my eyes and open them again. I look out Ron's car window and see the wild, vast southern hill country abundant in dark green native brush. The car tilts vertically as we drive up a tall hill. At the top of the hill, the whole world opens up, revealing large Spanish contemporary houses nestled between acres of land. The sprawling city springs forth from the rocky terrain and hunter green brush like an urban oasis. The Austin city skyline appears straight ahead of us under a midday sky.

"Quick, take a picture!" Carmen blurts out before taking a picture with her phone herself.

We enter the city limits with bated breath as the road carves into endless hills and slopes. The pressure in the atmosphere changes the further we get to the city.

We enter the city on road 290, behind Lake Austin. Austin, Texas, is the fourth most populous city while Houston is the most. Even so, Austin is a lot less crowded and stuffy. We pass through historic Texas landmarks, stadiums, parks, and baseball fields. I breathe in the hot and wet tropical climates of the Northeast city side. Red clay soils under bright green hedges and trees brighten the landscape. It feels fresh and vibrant city life.

"Look, there's the Capitol building." Carmen points to a large historical dome-roofed building in the distance.

"And right on that side over there is Sixth street."

"Where?" Ron asks with hands on the wheel, focused on driving.

"Over there on that side." She taps on the opposite side of the Capitol building, but he can't see where she's pointing to.

"Wow!" I gaze at the two-to-three-story brick Victorian Buildings. The old city never left this modern time; it's actually still alive, bustling, and thriving as pool halls, pizzerias, bars, and night clubs.

"I used to come down to Austin with my family all the time," Ron confides.

"I love Austin." Trent's head is turned to look at the sights.

"Really?" I look at Ron, and he glances at me.

"Yeah, my grandpa used to live here."

"Oh." I say, surprised.

***

My mind races back to 2017, right before the flood and the year after Trump was elected in office. A solar eclipse appeared near our sky, for who or what, can't know…

Five months later, in August, Hurricane Harvey and Ira created a massive flood over our community, leaving us homeless and jobless. At the time, my dad had a used boat and his high-axle truck, which he used to save the elderly in low-lying areas from the flood in the back of Kingwood.

I respect my father and hate him at the same time. My dad is old school, sadly. He keeps a licensed shotgun under his bed for hunting wild game and unruly boys who try to break into our home.

***

I stare out the window with deep melancholy as we drive through the metropolitan streets to the outskirts of the city.

"Yeah, before he passed." Ron looks out into the street before the light we stopped at turns green.

"Oh... I'm sorry."

"It's okay; I was like 14 when he died."

I feel a small pang inside my heart. I understand, flashbacks of my grandmother's funeral confront me. Unlike Ron, I still miss my grandma, my abuela, and I

171

think about her all the time. I can't even watch the Disney movie, Coco, without bawling uncontrollably.

We drive around through old-world and metropolitan streets until we pass the bridge over Lake Austin. The GPS map leads us in a neighborhood just outside the city and finally stops at a hotel that doesn't appear like a Hilton.

"Okay, we're here." Ron announces.

"Uh, no it's not..." Carmen looks at the old flat-top building. "It doesn't even look like it's open."

"Well, the map is telling me this is it."

"What!? No." Carmen pulls out the hotel reservation on her phone.

"Wah... wah... wahhhhh." Trent lets out.

"Well, I don't know what to tell you."

"This is on South Congress St." She taps on her phone. "Our hotel is on 7712 E. Riverside Drive." Carmen starts to get annoyed.

"Oh shoot. For real? Now you tell me."

"Let's just park around the corner. I saw a shop I want to check out."

11
La Alma

"Where are we going?" I ask Carmen, but my question remains unanswered as we traverse between urban and suburban backyards just outside the city. We parked along the curb bordering wire fences.

"Seriously, where are we going?" I ask again.

"I have no idea where Carmen is taking us," Ron walks by my side.

We walk in silence towards the end of the block to find a small tucked-away building. You would miss it unless you knew where to look, embedded under growths of ivy and shaded underneath oleander trees. Above the door hangs a wind chime and a small square, white sign that reads: The Herb Bar. I look back on the side, and there is another sign on the painted tile that says, "Best place to cure what ails you."

"Ohhhh, okay."

"The Herb bar," Trent announces in his baritone voice.

"Finally, a good place to buy weed," Ron comments.

"Do they sell weed?" Carmen sounds incredulous as she heads toward the coral-red door.

"Not legally."

"What do they sell? Herbs and spices."

We open the coral-red door bordered by a teal doorway.

An intense waft of incense hits us as soon as we step onto the red brick fortifying the metaphysical shop. An oak bar with a tapestry of a Hindu goddess sitting on a lotus greets us.

"Ohhhh, it's a crystal shop," Ron walks around the bar to the right next to the precarious shelving of rows and assortments of essential oils in dropper bottles. To the left, there's a Boho-glam doorway and wall with mirrors that opens up to a separate room for loose-leaf herbs and teas. I look inside to read the labels of tea but the lettering on the jars of tea is too small and far away for me to read.

"Do you need help finding anything?" A woman behind the counter asks.

"No, no, thank you. I'm just looking." I look down to the left. A potted snake plant in a woven pot holder sits on a worn Persian rug.

I walk further towards the back of the store. I enter a small closed-off glowing space filled with books on mismatched shelves about the Metaphysical. I read the covers on some of them, the Four Agreements. (that's a good eye-opening read.) Chakra healing, Herbiary, Astral Projection, and Goddess Training: become the women you were meant to be. Star-shaped lanterns and sphere paper lanterns illuminate the room with a warm glow.

I glance over the books. I am curious to buy one, but the price of the books outweighs my interest. To the right side of the small room, holistic shampoos, conditioners, and goat milk soap bars line the shelves. The smell is lovely but slightly irritating. I slip out of the back room and walk towards the center of the store. Short and square shelves with smudges of sage line the hallway.

Blue sage smudge $17

Desert magic sage $13

Blue sage & palo santo smudge $19, Prosperity smudges $19 and two other smudges at the bottom that are unlabeled next to incense holders.

The magic of the little shop continues as I head into the last room in the middle. The low ceilings contribute to a cozy cottage feel. The doorway in the center opens up to a crystal room.

It's a warmly lit room with tables all around with small clear glass bowls filled with all different types of crystals. Inside the bowls, like paper flags on potted plants, are assorted pink and yellow lists; each one describes the properties of the crystal it's next to. I used to be unaware of crystal names and crystal healing. I just liked collecting pretty and strange rocks as a child. My first crystal given to me was from my fourth-grade teacher, to be held like a worry stone. It was a smooth tiger's eye, formed like a sloped pyramid. I carried its glossy gold and umber colors everywhere, only to let it rest on my desk, collecting dust. To this day, it remains tucked away in a trinket box within my mom's storage closet.

Carmen and Ron coincidentally meet me in the room.

"Look, there's Tourmaline, moonstone, amethyst, amber, carnelian, and tiger's eye." Carmen sifts through the bowls with curious eyes, grabs a sunstone, and rubs the pink-sand colored stone between her hands.

"I already have crystals at home, but I wanna see if they have any I don't have." She wanders around to the right with her eyes down, slowly hovering and inspecting each crystal.

Ron stays by my side to look at some of the crystals with me. I take inventory in my mind of the crystals I already have: a small pack of assorted crystals I bought from a bookstore for chakra healing. Hmmm... I have amethyst, aventurine, rose quartz, and tiger's eye. Plus, whatever random pretty rock I picked up as a kid. Now all laid out and labeled before me, with their metaphysical properties listed below, crystals, exotic crystals. Some I've only read about.

"You know some people think that crystals are witchcraft and are evil," I say to Ron over my shoulder.

"Yeah, I don't think so. I don't think they're evil at all. They're natural elements made by God. Why would they be?"

I understand him.

"Yeah, some people are just afraid of what they don't know." I cancel my search and strike up a conversation with one of the employees. She's blond, clad in a comfortable, light blue sweater. "Can you believe that some people think that owning crystals is witchcraft and a sin?"

"Oh... umm yeah, I guess some people are just ignorant... Actually, in Revelations, it talks about the new Jerusalem. 'The foundations of the wall of the city were adorned with every kind of jewel.'"

Her smile tilted up to one corner, almost like she was ready for this conversation.

"And even before then, during the Old Testament, they fashioned crystals into a breastplate with 12 stones, each to represent the 12 sons of Israel. The high priest used it to receive divine guidance from God." She waves her hand in the air to express its revered spiritual likeness.

"Oh... oh wow... that's awesome." My eyes light up, and I can feel my heart glow with wonder.

"I think I remember reading something like that."

I look back at the array of crystals behind me, curious now to find the 12 stones used in the biblical breastplate.

"If you need help finding a stone to help you talk to God, just let me know. I'll be right here." I hear her mirth in the tone of her voice.

"Haha, if I do, I'll let you know. Thank you." I nod my head in respect.

I look back at the crystal bounty, and one particular crystal catches my eye.

"Woah..." I grab a smooth dodecahedron. "I've never seen this crystal in stores before." I rub my thumb over the deep maroon hues.

"What is that?"

"It's a—"

"Oh, a garnet." Ron interrupts my explanation.

I look at the purple slip. "It says it's for protection against psychic attacks and for health, passion, and energy." It could be useful for my mental health and ignite passion between me and Ron. Maybe I'm not doing this relationship thing right with him, anyway today is Valentine's day.

I gather my selection and complete my purchase at the oak bar at the front next to a few small novelty, spiritual items. The friendly Austonian woman checks me out. And so begins my journey into spirituality.

My friends and I regroup towards the exit.

Carmen closes the shop door behind us.

"What'd you get?" I look at Carmen, who's holding a paper bag in a clutch.

"Margret's moving into a new place, and she's really into astrology and birth charts now. So I got her an astrology candle to clear negative energy."

Margret... Hearing Carmen utter her name brought up memories of her ferociousness. I haven't said a word to her since we graduated high school.

Margret Cortez, our friend since middle school. Carmen's family and her family became close when Carmen's mom started dating and had a child with Margret's dad. They became as close as sisters and fought like sisters too. Since graduation, they have fallen out, but throughout high school, Margret and I have always been in and out of friendship.

The worst fight we ever had that really showed me what she was capable of started in middle school.... It was late September of our 7th grade. Summer had just ended, but the heat still lingered. It was two weeks before our middle school dance, and Carmen introduced me to her new boyfriend, Hector. We hung out after school, ventured underneath the roads through tunnels and trails to the nearby Muslim-owned corner store, and bought sour candy with our leftover lunch money.

One night after school, Hector called me and asked me who I liked and if I'm going to the dance with anyone. At the time, I had the biggest crush on Derek Halls. Derek was suave and funny, and he was popular with all the girls at our school, and I believe he's already married now, but at the time, I had a huge crush on him. Anyway, I never told anyone I liked Derek, not even Carmen or Margret, cause I knew they would eventually get to Derek and ruin everything. And yet, I told Hector. He said I should ask him out. I told him not to tell anyone, Hector promised he would keep it a secret. The next day at P.E., without warning, the girls ripped into me with venom.

"What is wrong with you???"

"You're such a bitch."

"We are not hanging out at the dance anymore."

"I can't believe you would do this to me..." Carmen held out her arms like I had stolen something from her.

"I f***ing hate your lying ass." Margret said with a growl, her black hair flew as she crashed her leg into my side like a wild horse.

I left school that day with a bruise on my side where she kicked me, a reminder that our friendship was ruined.

7th grade was the absolute worst. I was clueless as to why they betrayed me. The next day when I asked why they were mad at me, Carmen crossed her arms and said, "Don't play dumb, you know what you did," she turned away from me.

"I don't want to talk to you anymore, stay away from me." She gave me the cold shoulder for the rest of the year. I was, however, on Margret's shit list. She never let up her bullying; I was assaulted by her so often that the P.E. coach saw me crying in the locker room with bruises and asked me over and over.

"Who did this to you?" but I wouldn't tell her who it was. I didn't want my friends to get in trouble, if I could even call them friends anymore.

The abuse wasn't just physical; it was verbal too. I was called a "slut" or "f***ing puta." I was completely miserable and naive as to why I deserved this treatment. Was it because I was mixed race? Was it because I didn't know Spanish fully? Was it because I liked anime?

I was ultimately shunned and ostracized from their friend group, but eventually, I found new friends to sit with at lunch in 8th grade.

After high school started... During the first week, when class was over, I descended the concrete stairs in the commons and looked up to witness Carmen and Margret at the bottom of the flight. The expressions on their faces looked full of regret, and they welcomed me with open arms, telling me how sorry they were for the way they treated me.

It turns out Hector had lied to Carmen.... Hector created this deception that I liked him and asked him to the dance. Total middle school bullshit, and the only reason he confessed was that he saw how brutally they treated me.

I hugged them and sobbed sighs of relief into Carmen's arms.

"We're sorry we didn't believe you. It was Derek you liked this whole time."

"Yeah, I'm not a slut..." I outcry as tear droplets spring in my eyes.

"No!" "No, you're not." It's as if they'd let out apologies they buried inside for so long.

"I would never go after your boyfriend." I urged, if only I'd known to say that sooner. I hugged her even tighter as I buried my head in her shoulder until I couldn't see the outside world anymore. I felt her chest quake and heave with contrition. "Ughhh... I really hate boys..." Carmen sighed.

—

"Oh yeah, I told Margret you're in a relationship with Ron now." I come out of my flashback in shock.

"You—you WHAT!? You told her!!??" My jaw drops. "You, yo, y—"

"Yeah, she couldn't believe it, and then she started laughing. She said 'you're dating that nerd Ugh

Seriously! Ron Smithing'?" Carmen copied Margret's snarky voice.

"But, she also said you'd be sweet together."

"Oh, great... how is she?" I can't tell if I'm being sarcastic or not. I look at Carmen as we linger on the overgrown street corner as cars drive by.

"She's fine, she's gonna start an internship from Lone Star College."

"Good for her." I look down as we walk down the street.

"Yeah, we haven't been talking recently. The last time I called her was after you left our last hangout. But I promised her I would buy her a souvenir from Austin." She raises up her paper bag with the Virgo Candle inside.

Huh, I'm not surprised Carmen thinks Margret needs her energy cleared with a candle. It's been four years since we graduated, but she hasn't invited me to hang out since, but I didn't reach out to her either... Too many bad experiences with her.

Ron glances at my small paper bag. He nudges my arm as we walk side by side.

"Hey, what'd you get?"

"I got a Garnet, sunstone andddd... The crystal that makes you fertile." I bring it up to tease him.

"Whatttt?? Aw nooo." Ron teases back by shoving me lightly.

"I got it for creativity; it's a carnelian." I whine to him.

"Please don't get pregnant, Adriana... I'm not ready to have kids." Ron whines back. Carmen laughs at us.

I twist my face. "Yeah, no, me neither... In this economy?"

"Heck no, I'm not ready to be a fath—" "Ughhh, shut-up! Ya'll are both gay." Trent groans, annoyed at the conversation.

Carmen tosses back a laugh. But Ron pulls me into a side hug and kisses my forehead as we make our way past the neighborhood streets to my car. I'm for sure not planning on making a baby. But just being here with him is nice, exciting, and cozy. I'm glad I can just be myself around him. He's someone who gets my weird jokes, someone who shares the same goofy humor. I'm truly grateful for Ron, for being my first healthy relationship.

Once we take up space in my car, we update the coordinates to the right hotel and make our way down Congress Street.

The correct address wasn't that far away. Everything's connected in the city. The sun sets when we arrive. We enter a curving parking lot with well-trimmed yellowish grass strips surrounding the area. We park in front of the hotel's tennis courts. The sun's golden-orange radiance casts the city in a warm glow. Carmen steps out of the car.

"Okay, I am going to check-in. You guys stay here."

"Okay," I say, out of formality.

She walks past the back of the car towards the Hampton Hotel. When we lose sight of her, Ron opens the driver door.

"Trent, let's start unloading the luggage..." Ron looks back at Trent before leaving the car.

"...Rog." Trent lifts his bones up to exit the car. Trent says Rog, like Rod-ge, a shortened version of Roger.

I stay inside to gather my purse.

"Woaahhh.."

"Wow..." I look up to see Ron and Trent staring in awe at the horizon. It is a pretty sunset. Confused at their new reaction to the sky, I look down to slip on my maroon pointed shoes.

Someone abruptly starts banging on the driver's side window. I look up to see the source of the banging.

"Adriana, come out! You gotta see this." Ron slams his open palms on my window.

"... What?" I say under my breath. I open the car door and step out; the sight of it takes my breath away.

The horizon behind the tennis court and past the trees opens up, and the world is kissed by a violet light under the sunset, over the skyline.

"Ohhhh..." I gasp at the wondrous light. It's so beautiful; it's as if heaven itself crowned the city of Austin in a violet ray of light. Bathed in its hue, we start unpacking the car and head to the Hampton Hotel's entrance.

Carmen meets us up at the doors with a rolling bell-hop cart. The hotel room is decent. A one-bedroom with basic amenities. A window with a view of skyscrapers in the downtown Austin area. The warm glow of the sunset settles on the two beds in the room, the one room. I stare at the two queen beds separated by only 4 feet of space, leaving no privacy for me and Ron...

This could be a problem.

We unpack quickly and leave the hotel in hopes of exploring the city and its secrets. I wanna see why Austin is so weird, as I've been told.

We drive up through and under the hilly outskirts of the city, down roads that weave through the suburbs. The houses range from tall, luxurious modern homes to industrial chic, with neon shabby chic shacks interspersed in between. We cruise though these neighborhoods, ogling at just how different each house was. New homes made from up-cycled, steel shipping containers, small modern flat-top homes. Some even had murals and graffiti painted over them. We even pass by an ocean-themed house with a giant, blue, 3-D cut-out octopus taking over the front of the house.

"Wow, look at all these different homes." Ron glances at the neighborhoods while at the wheel. The HOA here is super chill here I'm guessing.

"Holy shit! Yeah, these f***ers are gentrified as hell." Trent acknowledges the state of Austin's housing crisis.

Ron drives up a hill as he rounds the bend. "Let's all just split the price on one of the houses here."

"Yeah, I'd be down." Trent looks at him though the rearview mirror with a playful grin.

Carmen switches windows to view the houses on Trent's side. "Oh yeah, some of these homes are really nice, me and Hassan thought about moving into a house a block over from here. But it was too expensive for even both of us."

I remember how when I was asked where I wanted to move out I always answered Austin, Texas. It was close enough to still see my family, and far enough away from them so I wouldn't have to run errands.

"I wanna move here so badddd." I tapped on my window in desperation. In my head, I knew though, I wanted to move out more than move in anywhere... Too many bad memories. In fact, I'm scared of the things I can't remember. I press my head so hard on the glass window and look at my reflection and the view outside at the same time.

"I would split a house, but I need to go back to school in Houston." Carmen glances down before turning to wistfully stare outside.

I think about splitting a house with just me and the boys there, ummm... That would never work, Not unless we got physically married and divided up the house.

We decide to start our tour of the city by eating dinner first. Carmen insisted on this restaurant called El Alma.

El alma is the Spanish translation for the soul. It's also a popular Spanish name, I think it's a beautiful name. We get turned around and miss the entrance, but we finally spot the white, pueblo-style building at the curb on Dawson street.

We park in the cramped parking lots along the edge of the building. On the outside, El Alma doesn't look like much. You'd miss it if you didn't know where to look. It almost looks like a plain ol' strip mall.

I look up to view a hanging retro sign with red and green neon lights that read, El Alma in Spanish calligraphy. Underneath it reads cafe y cantina.

As we stroll around the corner to the front entrance, the place had a vintage vibe. A long forest green banner sign outlined in red neon lights read; *'rooftop-patio bar - happy hour'*. I turn my head up but I don't see any chairs or living spaces on the roof.

"Are you sure about this place, Carmen?" I am a little uncertain about this cantina.

"No yeah, trust me on this place, it's soooo good. Me and Hassan used to eat here all the time. They even have Vegan options."

"I'm sure it's good." Ron assures.

We step inside and we're instantly teleported to a gorgeous restaurant in Cancun Mexico. The classic red tile, white walls, hanging woven baskets over each light fixture and retro Mexican styling give life to the cantina.

Carmen steps up to the reclaimed stained wood center to request a table.

"Hi, do you have a table for four, please?" a young Mexican woman in her 20's looks up from her list. "Do you have a reservation?"

"Can you hold on for a moment please?" she squeaks.

Carmen turns around to face us. "Oh, crap we need a reservation." She panics under her breath.

"Oh, hold on." The hostess at the desk furrows her freshly picked brow.

"We have a spot that's available. It's on the rooftop. Is that okay?"

"Yes, that's perfect." Carmen sighs with relief.

"Okay! Someone will be with you in a moment."

We walk around to the left to wait at the bar. Beyond the cherry red wood-stained bar lies a sight to behold: a genuine rock wall draped in ivy, aloe, and succulents growing in the crevices.

"Oh, wowww..." Is it a waterfall fountain? Upon further inspection, I spot a staircase embedded in the rock that leads you upstairs to the rooftop patio. The staircase is bordered by a black iron railing with black candle holders in between rails. The candles are even assorted in the wall. I glance over the bar on the right and notice that the rock wall is divided from the bartender by a black iron woven wall piece.

The atmosphere of the entire restaurant sparks flashbacks of another glowing earthly restaurant I visited when I was a teen.

The boys line up with Carmen at the bar. I stand near a green abstract painting, facing the wall, enchanted by it, wanting to enjoy the ambiance of the rock under small glowing lights.

Carmen and Trent gently walk up to me with cocktails in hand.

"Here, try this." She hands me a glass with a clear liquid with lime pulp.

"What is it?"

"It's ranch water. Just try it. It's good."

I relent and take a sip from the tiny black straw. It's tangy and burns smooth.

"Mmmm, refreshingly alcoholic."

"See, I told you you'd like it." She brings it back to her mouth.

Trent enjoys a mango-colored drink. I love mangoes, and I want to ask him for a taste.

"Can I try some of yours?" I wave my pointer finger at Trent's drink.

"Uh, no." He turns away from me to angrily sip the mango blended drink. I figured he'd say that.

"Table of four?" A hostess appears from the kitchen.

"Oh, yes," Carmen says lightly and steps forward. She leads us up the enchanting rock wall staircase to the door that leads to the secret rooftop patio. It's like I'm being led up the staircase in a tower to see the Spanish princess.

The hostess opens the glass door with a twinkling sound of a wind chime. And we are led down a narrow white wooden pathway next to a lifted platform. I can see the metal chairs taking up space on the raised platform behind a railing with woven metal wire, framed with wooden rails. It must be two feet, or more off the floor as we rise to it from a small staircase. The hostess seats us at a table right in front of the entrance of the stairs. (No wonder this table was available.) I absorb the light, clean, white surroundings. I understand why I was unable to see the tables from the street; there are several sections of 8-foot walls separating us from the front of the building. I twist my head around to see that the walls opened up between a lattice wall to a view of the city and a tall 8-story glass building. You could view the city from a living space with cushioned benches and a hemp rug in the middle.

After entertaining the view, I settle in with the rest of the group. I look up to see the tables behind us shaded by beige umbrellas. The sun is almost fully set behind the skyline, leaving a faint glow in the sky. A waitress turns on an outside standing steel heater next to us. Strings of luminescent light bulbs light up the area simultaneously. A kind young waitress with a blond ponytail opens her notebook and looks at us ready to take our requests.

"What can I get started for you?"

"I'll have a water."

I look up at her.

"Me as well," Carmen follows.

"Water."

"Same."

"Okay, four waters. Any appetizers y'all would like to start out with?"

We all exchange glances at each other, all of us curious but not willing to buy apps. Carmen does ask for salsa verde and queso for our chips. The server dashes away, leaving with her swaying pony.

"This place looks amazing," Ron exclaims as he reclines back in his chair, tilting it back on its legs.

"Yeah, good job. You picked a good spot, Carmen."

"Hehe, shut up," she chirps, then glances down in embarrassment. "You haven't even tried the food here yet."

"This place does have four stars on Yelp," I guess Trent did his research.

The waitress comes back with our drinks, and we make our orders.

I get the Tacos al Pastor. Trent orders a side of their fried plantains accompanied by a tall frosty marg. Ron doesn't get anything but asks for another plate. I know I'll end up sharing my tacos with him. Carmen then orders a plate of veggie enchiladas with tomatillo sauce and a bloody Maria.

The observant waitress comments on how good the enchiladas are here before dashing inside.

I observe our surroundings. The cantina becomes increasingly more busy as the night moves in.

I tune into the Latin music they play from the hanging speakers. I daydream of nights spent at my aunt's house in south Texas. My aunt Flores fires up her taco cart. It wasn't a taco truck; it was more like a cart with a flat iron grill and stove stops on the side for Frijoles rancheros and a counter to load grilled onions, cilantro, and lime. Her street tacos are some of the best tacos I've ever had. Their backyard was where I first discovered alcohol in the form of lemon Smirnoff ice. I don't know if it's a Mexican thing or just our family thing, but my tíos love Smirnoff ice and Coronas.

In the corner of my eye, I see the waitress come in with our food towering over us before resting on the table. Carmen thanks the waitress and places a $10 bill under the plate after the waitress leaves.

"It looks delicious," Trent remarks on his steaming blackened plantains.

"Mmm... It looks like it came from a magazine." Steaming hot plates of Mexican cuisine were laid out before us. The start of the evening looked promising. The novelty of the food fades when I remember I have to share my tacos with Ron.

I disappointingly hand him his share of tacos. He NEEDS to get a job.

"Mmm..." Carmen closes her eyes in absolute bliss from her green enchiladas.

"Is it good? It's vegan, though, right?" Ron tilts his head in surprise before closing a bite around my taco.

"Oh wow." "This is... wow."

"Too good for words?"

"Mmmhmm," he says with a mouthful.

I join him and eat a bite. It's amazing, the pork complements the pineapple, an unusual but delicious combo. The flavor profile of the spices, joined together by the onion, cilantro, and lime, unleashes a new level of flavor. "Oh my god. It's so good."

"See."

"Mmm... It's like a party in my mouth."

"Tss... infidel, pork is strictly Haram." Trent confronts me, but he can't even roll his 'r's so he says (Ha-Ram).

"I'm just trying to enjoy my food here, TRENT. I'm not Muslim, and neither are you—Officially." He grunts, but I think he giggled.

I think I know why he wants to be Muslim... He wants multiple wives... Tch... Polygamy...

I'm pretty sure he knows... Jesus was also a prophet in the Quran.

We finish our meal. God, Trent's plantains were good. I had to get Carmen to ask Trent for some, and she gave me half of hers. Trent's biased for Carmen but prejudiced against me, so I gotta bribe him or make a trade if I want anything from Trent. I hope to one day come back to El Alma; I'll remember to buy the grilled, sugar-crusted, marshmallow-topped plantains, so delicious.

The perky waitress addresses us once more before leaving El Alma.

12

6th street nightlife

I look in the bathroom mirror to cleanse the oil from my face and reapply light makeup. I'm not that self-conscious with my friends, but for occasions like this, it's best to look your best. Even if my makeup runs, I'll know I had a good time messing it up.

We cruise through the vibrant city night to a parking garage just three blocks away from 6th street. The car experiences turbulence driving over 10 mph through city streets with slow bumps towards the entrance of the garage. We split the bill on a parking spot, and the machine hands Ron a small paper ticket. It's dark outside, but the parking garage is flooded by blinding white lights.

Before we can exit the garage, Ron looks around panicked and pats himself down.

"What's wrong, babe?" I ask him.

"I can't find the ticket."

"WHAT?" We say in unison.

"Ughhh... You just had it!" I yell. Meanwhile, I see Trent dip his head and turn around in a single movement.

"You just had it, Ron!" "I know!" He yells back as he frantically searches every crevice of his clothes.

"Ughhh..." I groan. "Well, when's the last time you had it?" Carmen asks with her hands out.

"When we were in the car." Ron runs, no, he jogs back to my car in desperation.

"God Ron, what is wrong with you?!" I yell in his direction. I am low-key furious right now. How on earth are we supposed to get my car back now? We walk, and then I pick up my pace to catch up to Ron.

"Did you find it?"

"No, it's not here."

"When's the last time you saw it?"

"In the car when they handed it to me, and then I put it in my pocket."

"It must've fallen out of your pocket, dude." Trent cocks his head to look down.

Carmen checks herself as well and dips down to hold her knees as she looks for our lost ticket. Ron closes my car door, and we follow Trent's footsteps. We all have our heads down looking in different areas.

"Look, here it is— Oh," "wait."

"What? Is that it?" Carmen asks as she pulls her hair from her face as she stands up.

"It's someone else's ticket."

"Well, it's their loss." Trent kicks a pebble.

"Yeah, let's keep it in case we need it." "Ok."

"But this isn't our ticket, how will this let us out?" Trent reasons.

"It doesn't matter now, just keep it, maybe it'll take it," Carmen looks outside the garage, annoyed. We take the unclaimed ticket and waltz towards the city streets.

"Wait, let's not go to Sixth street yet."

"There's this bar I want to go to."

Ron opens up his phone. "What's it called?"

"It's called ummm... uh — It's an arcade inside a bar."

"Cidercade?" Trent interjects. He's walking on the grass next to Carmen.

"Uh, yeah, I've been to Cidercade, they have more games but the beer is average." She waves her hand flat, to convey its mediocrity.

"Cidercade is like Chuck-e-cheese's but with beer." "Oh!" Carmen snaps her fingers. "It's called Recess."

"Ohhhh, Yeahhhhh..."

I watch over Ron's shoulder as he types it into his phone, walking almost into the street to the left.

"Well, we're going the wrong way."

"What?"

"Recess is on sixth street."

"We need to go back and make a left."

The group does a 180 and heads over to our first stop, walking together in unison.

"I've never been to an arcade bar before." I announce.

"You mean Barcade." Trent jaunts with one foot hitting the pavement and one in the grass.

Our bodies cast long, lanky shadows across the street.

"It's fun," Carmen replies in a high pitch.

"They have pinball machines, skee ball, racing games. While they serve you beer— It's not super fancy, but they have some good beer."

"Do they have cocktails?"

"Hmm... I'm sure they do."

We walk past a man eating a hot dog and walk further to see a hot dog cart.

"It's not that much further, take a right over here." Ron calls out.

As we turn a busy street corner, the buildings climb high, ascending to touch the sky. Of the white and rust-red buildings, the stylings are Victorian, gilded age, and some modern buildings.

The Austin city streets are a collage of different eras. I notice the people here are just as varied. As we walk past a man wearing a bedazzled blue cowboy hat with beaded fringe and matching boots.

It's funny when I'm in Houston; I always see these shirts that say "Keep Austin Weird" with smiley faces over bright tie-dye shirts. And yet, now that I'm actually here, I don't see any of the people wearing them. I only see the shirts in the storefronts of tacky gift shops.

The dark blue of the night slowly turns to black as the night arrives at 6:18. It's pretty cold out now; I'm glad I brought my brown knitted beanie and my knit scarf. There are vendors on the city streets selling bouquets of roses.

I can hear the distant sound of a live band playing a cover of the song *Crimson and Clover* by the Shacks, but in their own alt-rock style. I glance at the street lights; I look at my reflection in the shop windows—the cold air turned my nose pink. A certain air of romance lingers in the streets, gently kissing my cheeks.

It's enough to make me hold on to Ron tighter; I sigh.

"OH, I can see it, Recess, it's right over there." Carmen points to the neon sign for the bar; it reads "Recess. Arcade Bar." with the 'C' in Recess shaped like Pac-Man, and the other letters are formed with Pac-Man dots. The address reads 222 over the red brick arches to the left side.

We enter through the narrow archways made of brick. It's not modern at all. Once we step in, it feels like walking into a '90s arcade, not refurbished '90s but old, like it hasn't changed since 1996. The ceilings are square tiles like the ones in classrooms but painted black. The floor is a dark cement color, and the walls are made of brick. The entire bar is only illuminated by neon lights from light-up beer signs and the lights from the arcade games.

As we walk to the island bar in the middle of the building, I can feel my feet come up with more pull; the floor is a nice peppered wood, but sticky. Carmen waves over the bartender.

"What are you getting?" Ron asks her first.

"Mmm... Just a beer; they have two dollar beers here." She points to the hanging sign. Everyone looks up; the sign reads: "$2.00 dollar drafts, every day, all day."

"Oh, nice."

"Sweet."

"It's not exactly the best beer, but for two dollars, it's great. It'll get you drunk for sure, though."

"Alright," Trent stands up straight from leaning against the bar. "Ya'll can go bar hop around Sixth street. I'll be here all night."

Ron laughs. Carmen grabs Trent's arm. "Noooooo! You can't stay here, you nerd. Come with us."

She lets him go. "There are other spots I need to show you." There's a pause in the conversation.

"I call Street Fighter!" Ron heads to the quarter machine and collects 10 dollars worth of quarters. Trent follows suit. Me and Carmen take our chances at skee ball. The classic game's pink neon lights illuminate our bodies. We go head to head in the game as we play skee ball side to side.

Carmen ends up winning in the end. "3,350! It's not as hard as I remember."

I look at my 1250 score. "Yeah, you beat me!" I laugh.

Carmen gathers her purse from the floor. "I love skeeball; I always used to play with my dad when he took me to Dave and Buster's." I think about her situation; it must've been hard for her and her sisters after her parents divorced when she was young. She must enjoy special moments with her dad a lot more than I do with my dad.

"Too bad there's no arcade prizes." I look towards the bar. "Like maybe not sticky hands or clap bracelets, but if I could get tickets to win a free shot—now that would work."

She smiles at my speculation. "No, I don't think they do that here."

"That would be awesome, though." We head over to where the boys are; their faces and fingers glued to the superheroes vs. Capcom game. Their fingers move over the joystick and buttons in a frenzy.

Ron plays as Zangief while Trent fights as Wolverine. Wolverine K.O.s Zangief after a fatal blow. After a few more two-dollar beers and all of our change is spent on games, we exit the bar-cade and head down the main 6th street.

"Is it this way?" I ask.

"What? The way to where?" Ron answers my question with another.

"What are we doing?" I ask; my brain feels a little tipsy.

"I don't know. What do you want to do today?" Ron asks again.

"I don't know. What do you want to do today?" I lean into him, grab his arm, and make us sway back and forth as we walk.

"I don't know. What do you want to do today?"

"I don't know. Wha—" "ENOUGH! We are going to a club." Carmen yells, with her phone in her hands.

We walk past a pink doughnut shop called Voodoo Donuts. Some of the beers on tap are really setting into my bones. I can't help but spontaneously start to sing.

"I don't practice Santeria! I ain't got no crystal ball." Ron starts to join in. He grabs my hand, and we start to skip down the street.

"I had a million dollars, but I spent it all..."

Now everyone is singing, even including Trent. A few strangers turn their heads to see who's singing. One guy raises his beer bottle to us, and another man hollers "Wooo!" Yeah!"

"If I could find that hyena and that sancho that she's found." "Yeahhhhhh sing it," a woman's voice cheers from afar.

"Well, I'd pop a cap in sancho and I'd slap her dowwwwnnnn..."

We continue to sing and tipsy turn about the street until we finish the first chorus at a random shop.

Trent relieves an exhausted laugh from his chest.

Ron smiles and hugs me.

"Oh," I look around, we stopped in front of a place called the Soho lounge. "Where are we going again?"

"I want to show y'all this club called the Voodoo room." She looks at our faces. "Or we could just go bar hopping on Sixth Street." Carmen says before letting out a small burp. " 'Scuse me." She squeaks.

"Yeah, let's check out the Voodoo room."

We stroll down East 6th Street for half a block until we reach The Voodoo Room. The hanging sign depicts a voodoo doll head with a grimace and two needles coming from its head like skull and crossbones. The building, in black and white, sports two large windows on each side of the door. It's so narrow that the entrance and windows dominate the entire front space.

We daringly walk inside the Voodoo room; the lights inside are dimmed with black walls and black hanging geometric chandeliers. Strobe lights dance and flicker across the bar. The music is blaring loud. They're playing a remix of Britney Spears' *"Hold it against me,"* but I will because I can't hear anything else but the music. I look around at the forming crowd of people around me. I focus on Carmen who's waving at me from the bar. Her mouth is moving but I can't understand what she's trying to tell me.

"What?" I yell at her with my hand cuffed over my ear.

She comes closer to me with both her hands cuffed over her mouth.

"I'm going to buy a drink, you want one?!" My ears adjust to the volume.

"Sure!" I yell back.

Carmen flags down a bartender. Miraculously the blaring music volume lowers enough for us to hear our own thoughts. Ron was about to whisper in my ear before he realized he can talk regular now.

"Damn, finally. They turned down the music."

"I'm not seeing that many people. Why would they have it turned on that loud?"

Ron shrugs his shoulders in his red plaid shirt. "I don't know."

My guess is they gotta play it loud so people from the street will get curious and walk in. Ready to get down to whatever song they're playing. There are so many bars on Sixth Street. There's practically a bar scene for everyone here.

From the corner of my eye, I see someone approach Carmen.

I glance sideways to see him. He's a slightly tall man, probably about 5.8. His face is rectangle shaped, and his skin is a sickly olive color. His hair is black and wavy with a noticeable five o'clock shadow.

He looks like a skeeze.

The lights from the club flash over his posture, with his groin jut out and his legs spread out, taking space.

"Hi, sweetheart," He crooned with a certain southern city suave. "You looking for me?"

He flips his hair and leans in to Carmen's space.

"No, actually, I was just trying to have a good time."

"Oh, baby, if you stick with me, I'll show you a good time." His eyes move up and down her body, but linger on her breasts for a little too long.

"Oh, are you trying to date me? Or are you just trying to have a good time?" She shifts her weight to one leg and leans against the bar. She appears to be offended, but also amused.

"Yeah, mamas, let me buy you a drink, I am Jonnie." He grins, revealing his sharp yellow teeth.

Carmen shakes her upwards open palm. "Oh, that's okay, you don't have to."

Jonnie invades her space, ducking his head close enough to almost kiss her. "Come on baby..." "Let me buy you a drink." He persists.

"I said NO, okay!" Carmen turns away from him to look at me.

"Hey, hey, I just offered you a drink!" His face riles up a fierce frown. "Is it because you're on a diet?..."

His smooth talk fades, as his true self comes to light.

"Uh huh, ha... Because..." He eyes her body up and down, enjoying but flicking off from her breast.

"You look enough..."

I gasp. Carmen turns around from me to face Jonnie.

"Excuse me!?" Carmen hisses.

He diverts his attention to his glass for a petty sip. and turns back to face Carmen. "You heard me sweetie, you look BIG enough."

Carmen gasps.

Hell no, he did not just call her that. I start to walk towards them but it's too late. Carmen pulls back her hand and releases the force of a slap so hard it jolts his face back and shakes the grease from his oily hair. A few people look back to see the commotion.

"HEY!" The bartender yells in our direction. I grab Carmen's arm.

"Let's go!"

I grab Carmen and run out the door.

"Ron, Trent, let's goooo!!!" I flee while dodging and ducking a new crowd of people entering the building. An angry bartender yells at us to leave. I look back at the scorned man; he's rubbing his right cheek. He looks guilty but hateful.

"Yeah, get outta here you f***ing BITCH!"

I glance back at the man.

Tch, scumbag... I think as I stumble over the sidewalk ledge.

As soon as me and Carmen exit the building, two exotic dancers climb up on platforms in the front windows and start their cabaret show in Emo heartthrob couture.

Inside everyone starts to hoot and holler as their half-naked bodies dance around poles in corsets and purple and green thigh-high socks.

"Wow, hahahaha, holy cow, I can't believe you slapped him!" I look at Carmen with wild eyes. I'm crouched over holding my knees, heaving and panicked.

Me and Carmen look around but Ron and Trent are still inside.

Carmen calls their phones for them to reveal themselves from the crowd. I'm standing on the sidewalk outside looking in, to see if I can see a glimpse of those knuckleheads.

Carmen calls Trent's phone.

"Yeah," Carmen relays the calamity. "He called me fat after I turned his ass down." She looks around as she puts her phone to her ear. "And then I slapped him." I hear loud music and laughing on the other side of the phone call. "I'll tell ya'll about it as soon as you get outside. Where are ya'll anyway?"

I can't help but look at her body. She's wearing a really sexy black tank top with a short sleeve black see-through sheen top over it. Carmen is a beautiful curvaceous woman but she's not obese.

The guy she slapped said she was big to get back at her for turning him down. Typical f*** boy move.

"How can a guy who looks like a rat with jaundice get to a girl who looks like you? You're a ten out of ten."

"Haha, whatever," she laughs and scoffs at me, her hand waving freely.

I swivel my head to see the dancers. One of them has long black flowing hair that drapes over her thighs as she beckons leering men into the entrance of the club.

Ron and Trent finally walk out of the V Room.

"Why are we leaving? The girls just got here," Trent has a wicked grin twisting his face.

"Ahemmm..." I pretend to clear my throat, raising one eyebrow at Ron (who's still staring at the girls) and stare him down.

"God, emos scare me..." I look at the girls with green and black leggings, swinging thigh highs, and black boots.

He notices and turns around, laughs, shakes his ash brown hair, and pulls me into a hug, squeezing my butt. That's when the cold settles in my bones. I can really start to see our breath in the wind when we speak. The clock on my phone shows 10:30. As the temperature decreases to 44 degrees.

We take our night to 7th street, to a classy, eclectic Mexican cocktail bar called Las Perlas. The boys order their favorite, Dos Equis. Carmen orders a spiced daisy margarita (it's funny because Margarita means daisy in Spanish.) I order a few Coronas and a plate of nachos from the taco truck on the lot. We spend that time outside the bar's courtyard at a picnic table regaining our energy by eating delicious barbacoa-loaded nachos. Carmen can't resist and orders more cheese sauce and picante sauce for everyone. We equate our alcohol intake with the same amount of lemon water from the waiter's pitcher. I don't wanna see this night end in vomit, especially on Valentine's day. I'm just worried that Ron will find out how I really feel about him. What if my feelings change tonight? I stare down into my bottle of Corona looking at all the savory foam around the inside of the bottle. The word 'Corona' is already starting to turn into a trigger word for people on account of the new virus in China.

"Come on, let's go! I wanna show you guys another place before they close." Carmen waves us down and leads the way out of the bar and down the street.

I look at the clock on my phone; it's only 11:05. "Yeah, I know, but this place might close early."

"Plus, it's a long way from here," she looks out at the low-key city streets. The buildings are only as high as 6-8 floors around here.

"Where are we going anyway?" Ron says apprehensively, while looking at his phone. The stoplight's red glow tints my glasses as we wait at the crosswalk.

"It's a surprise!—This way." We curiously follow her across the crosswalk. The temperature drops, our now hot breath from walking leaves puffs of white clouds in the air as we walk.

I try to keep up with them as they cross the street. "Ow," the pinch from my gray-tan-tight-high-heel boots leaves me behind the group. My feet are really starting to hurt from walking all night.

"What's wrong?" My boyfriend asks, trying to be caring.

"Oh, my feet hurt," I wince.

"Do you want me to carry you?" He chuckles. "Oh no, I'm fi—" but before I could say "I'm fine," he swoops me up in his arms.

"Ahhh, Ron, stop it, put me down!"

He picks me up in his arms like a gentleman picking up his lady so she doesn't step in a puddle. Trent and Carmen smile at us before, and before I know it, Ron is jogging with me in his arms.

"Ahhh," I scream halfheartedly. "Help!" I yell as I look back at the others, as they get smaller and smaller in view. The huff of hot air vapors clouds my glasses and his. Our innocence in puppy love gives way to a new type of love I feel for him.

I want to clean my glasses so I can see him better...
What is it? Hmm... Oh right. Brotherly Love.

At that moment, I knew it wasn't meant to last.

"Ohhhhhhh," I scream. "Hey guys—HELP!" I yell
as I look back at the others as they get smaller and
smaller in view. They are still walking.

"She's not your property!" Carmen yells to Ron.

After a while, Ron begins to huff and breathe like
he's out of breath. He finally puts me down behind a
fire hydrant and sits on it to catch his breath while
chuckling.

"I told you I was fine," I smile down at him and
lean down to kiss his mouth. His breath smells of beer
and fruit gum... He looks like he's past drunk already.
Ron and I wait for the others to catch up before
walking ahead.

Carmen's destination leads us to the west side of
the city. After passing four blocks, we reach the
underbelly of an overpass. We have to cross it, and yet
Carmen looks hesitant.

I look around and I realize why... Under the bridge,
there's a homeless encampment. Tents to the left and
to the right blow in the cold wind like little white flags
of surrender. Surrendering from life, or maybe from
their wife. Or just misfits... orphans, victims, drug
abusers, the unwanted and pregnant, the handicapped.
All gathered here in refuge, outcast from society or
maybe just by their family... It isn't uncommon to see

the homeless in the streets of Austin. Unlike Houston, the city of Austin allows homeless people to sleep and camp in public spaces. But I'm not sure allowing homeless people access to sleep in the streets is actually helping the problem. There has to be another way like recycling old materials...

"It's pretty sad to see them like this..." I confide in Ron, who's on my right.

"Yeah, someone should help them." We walk past the encampment with a feeling of unease. Ron lets go of my hand to clutch my arm as he moves closer to me, as if to protect me from any danger.

But before we completely walk past the underbelly of the overpass— A homeless man with a basket of pink and red roses appears from one of the tents.

"Roses, Roses for a dollah!" I turn around.

"Sir, sir!"

I let go of Ron's arm to walk further down with Trent and Carmen who are in front.

Ron stays back and turns to see the man with a bushel of plastic pink roses in his hand.

"A rose for your lady?" Ron walks up to the homeless man; he's a ragged mixed-race man with a scraggly beard and matted brown and gray dreadlocks underneath a white hoodie. He looks to be about in his late 40s. He wears brown army green pants and worn-out sneakers. I didn't expect anyone to come out of a homeless encampment, but he's here ready to pop out and sell some roses for Valentine's sweethearts.

I do believe we should help people in need. And anything helps, but some people are only a threat to themselves... My dad has this ideology about homeless people; that people shouldn't give them cash because they'll go and buy drugs with it... It's better to buy them a hot meal than the opportunity to feed their addiction. There have always been people like him. Yet, with new infrastructure and means of living, people like him should have a chance in the future...

I stare at them from a distance; Ron pulls out his wallet and gives the man a ten. The homeless man's jaw drops in shock and gratitude. And yet, he also seems very helpful.

"Oh... Lemme see if I got change."

"It's okay. Keep the change, my man... You deserve it."

"Here, Lemme give you te—" The homeless man starts.

—"No, it's fine, one plastic rose is enough for my lady." Ron nods to the man, like a cowboy tilting his hat.

"Thank you, sir," the homeless man calls out.

"You're welcome." Ron turns to glance at him with a benevolent smile warming Ron's cheeks before jogging back to me.

"Ey, Happy Valentine's day!"

Ron keeps walking toward me.

"For you, m'lady..." Ron hands me the clear plastic-covered fake rose.

"Ohhhhh. Thank you, my good sir—" I twirl the rose in my hand before planting a kiss on his cheek; our visible breath collides in the cold air. I don't look at Ron, but I keep talking, "Do you think they're keeping us poor, just so we can become the zombies..."

"Yeah, people love to live out fantasy."

"Absolute trash mentality..." Ron says under his breath.

"I know, right, ugh."

"Like the capitalist pigs are keeping inflation so high to force women to become space whores on OnlyFans."

"I know it's disgusting."

We pass the overpass and arrive at a few buildings beyond. A modest white brick structure appears, adorned with royal blue awnings and accents in Chinese red and persimmon orange, creating a lively contrast against the white backdrop.

"Here it is," Carmen shivers. "Finally, hurry, let's go inside; I'm freezing my ass off."

I suddenly look up from staring down the road.

Ah Sing Den. A neon sign with a glowing martini with a cherry atop pronounces itself as vintage and Chinese, beckoning us in... I'm immediately intrigued. Chinese lion statues guard the front entrance as if to protect Ah Sing Den from evil spirits.

We are greeted inside by hosts; the lounge opens up to a fabulous mahogany bar with a dapper bartender dressed to the nines in a white collar with a blue tie and navy blue sleeve garters. Above him, persimmon orange-painted walls form mahogany-crowned arches showcasing shelves gutted with liquors and spirits.

Suddenly I'm nostalgic for an era I've never known.

"Oh wowwwww... This place is beautiful," I gasp as I look around the violet red curtains and paper fans + lanterns hanging down from the ceilings. I'm in absolute awe of the Chinese-American vintage glamour.

The server seats us in the back; the room is set up like a closed-off speakeasy with violet red Chinese lanterns hung from the ceiling and carefully placed Chinese ornate wooden dividers between tables.

"Oh my god..." Trent trails off his sentence like he was about to say, "I love this place."

"It's so beautiful..." Carmen pulls out her phone to take a picture.

"It's like a fairy tale..." Ron looks around; we are seated. Carmen and Trent are seated at a booth side, and me and Ron are seated table side. Trent orders a plate of edamame for the table. A server hands us our menus.

We take a moment to look at the menu... I order a drink called Malibu Sunkiss for 14 dollars. It better give me a beach flashback or I'm taking it back; I giggle to myself. Carmen orders Butterfly Kisses, Empress Gin, Gifford, Lichi-Li, Fuji, Apple Sake, lemongrass, grapefruit, Raspberry sage syrup, rose water-infused butterfly tea, furikake, wormwood bitters with egg white. Reading that cocktail felt like reading the ingredients for a potion of enchantment.

"Carmen, that drink sounds like an enchanted potion." I look around; I am already enchanted.

Trent simply orders special sake. Our orders come in. Oh, to love in this restaurant...

I want to say this night is perfect, but Ron just can't provide for me... I had to order my own cocktail and share... I recall his friends Moses.

"Hey, so how is Moses doing?" I strike up a conversation about their friend.

I am listening to Carmie talk about their friend Moses but I'm in and out of listening.

"Who was influencing him?"

"Oh well, some other guys at a party, and they had Xanax..." Ron had stated.

"Yeah, it's becoming an addiction for him," Carmen commented. Oh no, I think to myself.

"He needs to come clean," I declare.

"Moses is a hot odious potifer..." Trent slurs.

"A what?" laughing ensues.

"What am I— saying?" Trent slurs again.

"Yeah, well, Moses takes bribes and favors from rich older white women," Ron states. OH, there it is.

"Like a reverse sugar daddy," I blatantly speak, trying to complain about our situation as well.

"A sugar mama!" Trent blurts out, laughing with a yellow, persnickety, mischievous smile.

Our laughter turns into chuckles and groans now... Awkward... Oh god.

At that moment, our drinks come in. Thank god. My Malibu Sunkiss arrives as a coral peach color delicate drink, with a white flower garnish and a caramelized onion smell. It's fizzing like there are candy rocks at the bottom.

I take a sip... Mmm...

"It tastes like." Oh my gosh...

"What?" Carmen asks while Ron smells my drink. I let him have a taste.

"Oh." He smirks.

"Well..." Ron looks up at me, leaning his head back, extending his arm to grab my coat. His face expressioned with manly and machismo thoughts.

"...It tastes like pussy." I blurt. Laughter bursts from our table.

"Hoho hahahahaha... oh my god." I try to cover my frankness with laughter.

"I cannot believe— 'Ey waiter, our pussy tastes like drink!" Trent slurs. Ron bursts with laughter.

"—Shhhhhhhh, do NOT be rude," Carmen tames Trent's drunken self, she giggles.

"I cannot believe you said that out loud, Adriana." She laughs with her breasts bouncing slightly.

"Ppppbbt." Trent's spittle hits my face but he seems uncharacteristically happy with a beer to sip on.

"Well, I did order edamame for the table." Trent sits up tall to present himself.

13

Heaven's tears

A Night Inn

In a drunken haze, Ron and I bump heads that night. Nothing too surreal, or life altering. I'm not even sure he knows... He's heavily in denial about it though, buzzed off his mind and I am too. I spend the rest of the night tossing, turning, and heaving. Ron too.

After we leave our esteemed hotel, safe and sound, we arrive at a vintage shop clothing store called Flamingos. It looks like it has never changed since the 70s. I look like a giant hour glass with b cup boobs trying to fit into model size clothes.

I settle on a vintage purple and turquoise windbreaker.

Perfect.

Next door to Flamingos is Antone's record shop — it's the record store full of old CDs, Cassettes, even Vinyl. It feels as a record store should feel — the scent of old paper, vinyl sleeve and dust.

"Oh wow..."

They even have cool knick-knacks, shirts and lots of slick vinyl waiting to be discovered. The store specializes in soulful music. I pick up a CD from the Musical Youth. Now THIS is gonna inspire my poetry writing.

"Come on, let's find another record shop this one is more for soul and R&B." Says Ron.

Okay... Is that a problem? I chuckle to myself.

We make our way to another record store. It's larger but somehow the charm of Antone's Record store is missing here.

I find an album of The XX, one of my faves since high school.

The ride home is disheartening to say the least. I can't wait to bring my souvenir haul home. It'll be good to be back home with my family. I stare outside at the vast Texas plains before dozing off.

***

It's February 24th, and Carmen invites me and Ron to hang out in her attic room. I believe I'm not too shy to keep feelings bottled inside. It has been about three months for Ron and me. If I say the truth about my feelings, it'll be okay eventually... Anyway. I just know Ron is gonna be upset. I enter the room with unease, It feels like I have a ton of bad feelings waiting to be rolled off my chest.

"So well, I'm gonna go back to college eventually to become a social worker for children," Carmen continues with her train of thought, the beginning of which I missed in my own. I admire her for her dreams of helping children. Talking about our future like this will help me share my feelings too.

And if I say it... but, doesn't he?

"—*I, i don't see us getting married.*" I blurt out, The look on his face looks pained but it's the truth. *My truth...*

Carmen covers her mouth. "I cannot believe You said that— in front of me."

"I know."

"—You feel like this?" He responds still in shock but a contemptuous tone in his voice.

"I am so sorry, Ron, It's just that's how I feel—it's the truth."

I should've said it in private... CRAP.

The room looks grayer than it ever did, and the weather outside is gloomy even though it's noon.

"We should—go home." Ron said while grabbing his things.

"Yeah, let's go, Ron." I need to talk to him, I thought to myself.

I take Ron home. The rain starts to *plip* *plop* from the sky as if my guardian angels were somewhere crying for me.

We arrive at his apartment building, where more droplets fall over the aluminum awning.

"Hey—I," Ron starts to speak.

"Stop, I just— I just don't see us being together like this." I stutter as my lips start to tremble.

"I know, Adriana, I know—but we can start over."

"No—not like this." I stop him as tears start to form in my eyes. *Why am I crying though?*

He leaps out from my car and into the street.

"Wait—" I hastily come out of the vehicle and run up to him with words ready in my mouth, waiting to be spoken.

I catch him under the rain. "I know sweetie, I know. Please," I stop him. "Please, just don't stop being my friend." I beg.

"I can't BELIEVE you're doing this." He stomps his foot.

"I know, I know." I tell him.

"Why can't we try some more?" he pleads.

"NO, I just I just don't think we're gonna last."

"Come on, Adriana." Ron caresses my face with his hand.

I know how to make him confess...

"Hav— have you ever loved anyone, more than me?" I ask the heart wrenching question with quivering lips and a broken smile.

His answer...

"Yes." A tear escapes my eye. I feel so used, but I wasn't used. *Or was I?* I did love him but just not in the way you love someone romantically.

I turn away from him and clasp my hand over my mouth.

"...Im sorry..." He apologies. "It's okay.. I'll still be your friend."

"Would you? I mean we'll still talk like we used too, right?"

"I care about you." Ron sad while looking down. "Please drive safe." He assures me.

I run back to my car and shut the car door with a loud crack.

This is why... This is why. Carmen was right.

Never date in the friend group. Now the next time we hang out, we'll be stepping on egg shells trying to duck and be delicate over anything that would upset him. Or dodging romantic advances.

It's never gonna be the same.

I bang my head against my black steering wheel and let out a severe crying fit. Unfortunately, I am scheduled to work at 3pm that day.

I knew it was over.

I think he knew it too.

I go into work after a quick shower, to drown my sorrows down the drain. It's not like me to behave like this, and to lead him on. I waited until after Valentine's to break up with him because I felt bad. It felt wrong. But what's worse, leaving them when you want to? Or when it's convenient?

The Covid scare has everyone in a frenzy at work. Doomsday preppers and hypochondriacs alike are clearing the shelves like never before. Medicinal items are becoming out of stock like Vitamin C tablets, inhalers, vapor rubs, pens, rubbing alcohol. Even the snake oil cures are high in demand. It's insane what a virus scare can drive people to do. Unfortunately.

Im bagging groceries as I overhear two customers discussing Covid-19.

"I heard It was a virus mutation that came from Wuhan China."

"NO, it's bigger than that! They were doing experiments on bats!"

"What?! Bats?"

"MmmHmmm, bats! Like I said, it's a sad and awful world we live in."

Bats, huh? I think to myself but I dismiss it as mere gossip. I'd better start researching articles and the news for more reliable info.

I look at the stockers coming out in the daytime like miserable young vampires just to re-stock items that are flying off the shelves but mostly toilet paper, I mean seriously??? Toilet paper? They have to re-stock it like every 12 hours now it seems.

The people just kept lining up and lining up to my register; it was so busy. One after the other, they piled their goods and supplies. I felt like a robot, working for only $9.50 an hour, but it would cost so much more all at once to have an actual robot work as a bagger. Why can't people just bag their own groceries? Some people are so entitled, I swear...

It reached a point at the height of the rush around 5:20. It was so busy that I felt like I couldn't stop, and the managers didn't have anyone to switch out for my shift break. They left me there alone to fend for myself. It got to a point where I couldn't hold it in anymore...

And so...

I pissed myself...

If I didn't know any better, I would've quit right then and there...

I use the restroom as soon as its time to clock out.

Another day, another shitting dollar. Before clocking out, I overhear the managers talking about *enforcing a 6 foot rule. And only having a certain number of people in the store now.*

Thank god.

I let out more tears in my car before heading home.

14

Our night

It's March 3rd, and Spring break is almost here, and I am so close to graduating I can feel it. One of our projects involved making a flying saucer spin around a baseball field. I'm not really into creating fake CGI UFOs over baseball fields. Just looking at it made me a little wary...

As soon as spring break rolls around the corner, Carmen invites me to hang out with her alone. We take my car to the nearest Wal-mart and load up on our favorite snacks and munchies before heading back to her place. I take out my Arizona Iced tea, a small salad, some beef jerky, and a package of chocolate Swiss rolls. We stay up late that night watching Youtube conspiracy videos for an hour about Spirit Science. It's an animated video series about the science of spirit, about the untold, foundations of religion, space, and time. The ideas they talked really came from outer space... The idea that men are from Mars and women are from Venus was taken quite literally. It also stated that when Mary became pregnant with Jesus, she and Joseph had created a new life through astral. The spirit of god was allowed into her womb. Just amazing, I am just in awe of such a theory.

I realized then and there, I wanna start meditating...

That night before I leave Carma's house I tell her, "wasn't that insane!" I make a mind blown motion with my hands over my head.

"Yeah I know, a lot of this stuff is just theory, and kind of... Cultish."

A valid point.

She then looked around the room, rubbing the newly forming crystals from her eyes.

Right then I knew, and I knew she knew. Children really are a blessing from God.

That night I leave Carmen's house at around 4am.

I just don't feel like sleeping...

So I drive around my house to find a raccoon...

A huge fat one, rummaging though our recycle bin.

"what the—"

I nervously wait inside my car until the fat raccoon decides to leave our garbage bins. My headlights shining on his fat rump, waiting for the banded criminal to leave.

Shit.

Raccoons are notorious for carrying rabies, but it doesn't seem rabid. It's best to play it safe and wait till he leaves. He does and carries on over to the next house, looking for garbage.

Spooky.

***

I kinda feel restless the night before my family's trip back to McAllen, south of Houston, north of South Padre Island.

"We can't find the tulips!" My mom, Cecilia, yells in a bustling kitchen.

"Cecilia, we forgot to pick them up from the store!"

"AY no!" My auntie, Ara, exclaims.

It's March 14th. It's my cousin Anita's birthday today. And lucky for me, it's also spring break for our college. There isn't a reason to be out, especially given how scary the news has been: the fires in Australia, California, the World War III scare, and now a new Virus.

I try to help around the house as much as I can by sticking gold Ferrero-Rocher chocolates onto a gold styrofoam cone with toothpicks to create a beautiful pink display for my Anita's 18th birthday. I take a picture of her pink backdrop and her name in gold. I'm not sure how, but all the pink hue from the decorations seemed to be tinted gray, more like a dusty rose gold color. Anita is very accomplished; she became her band's orchestra lead by her junior year! She walks past me with her school colored ribbons in hand.

"Wow, looks like our Maestr(a) is finally old enough to vote!"

"Yeah, hehe." She sheepishly admits.

"It's a big step for you—how do you feel?"

"It's good, I'm good, not something I'm used too, but I'm getting a lot more respect from my friends now."

"Yeah! You're awesome! You should be respected." I smile a half smile at her.

"AWe Sthaap." She waves her hand and disappears into her room.

I disappear into my *tia* Marie's room and prep my look. This has to be a good day. I wanna have a good day. I wanna forget all the bad and tragic happenings around the world. And make myself look beautiful, to remind myself and others too that I am happy again. I am growing and changing as well.

Once I am done with my make up. I step outside and I sit on the steps of a newly refurbished concrete semi-half porch. I watch brown lizards and blue-banded skinks dart across the white-hot quartz rock. A monarch butterfly flutters and stops and takes a sip of nectar from a purple flower. There is still love in the world, there is someone out there who really gets me, someone who will be my friend and lover.

Love is patient. Love is kind. It doesn't envy. It doesn't boast, it is not proud.

I remind myself, the next few parts of the verse that I tend to forget.

I look around to the front of the backyard, everything has changed since I was little. I used to play here in this backyard as a child with all my tias, playing in a plastic pool, rubber duckies bobbing in the grassy water. I was clean, whole, and pure; before iPhones or social media, life was abundant and natural...

On hot, dry summer days in the southern lands my abuela would fill her entire apron with tiny key limes from the key lime tree. Whenever they were in season, she would trade them for freshly picked guava fruits from her neighbor's house.

Oh, what time has stolen from us... I miss my grandma more and more each day.

"Hey Adri, we're singing happy birthday." My tia Ara startles me from my day dream.

"OH right!"

I pick myself up off the stoop and follow suit. To sing "Happy Birthday."

All her friends made a video compilation, expressing their appreciation of Anita's leadership and authority. And of how great of a musician she was.

Her birthday was a success, despite it all…

$$15$$

Essential worker

A day later, on March 15th, 2020, a loud, harsh tone plays on my phone, then on Jackie's phone, then on Anita's phone. A message reads: "Covid government shut down…"

"Did you hear?"

"It's beacuse of Covid 19."

"The governments shut down…"

I let my sister read out the government sent message.

I'm too horrified to read it out loud.

"Oh my gosh what is going to happen!" I blurt out, panicked. My mom shouts, "we are gonna be fine!"

"It's okay."

"Oh no, Oh no, you guys this is so bad." Anita shakes her head.

"I can't believe this is happening."

"Are we gonna die?"

"No, no, look," Jacqueline pulls up her phone.

"It says that only the old and those with weak immune systems such as heart conditions or weak constitutions."

"Weak constitutions?"

"— I'm not—"

"Huh?"

"I mean, compromised immune systems."

"It says some of us won't be able to work due to the shut down. But mandatory jobs are still effective?"

My sis, Jackie, turns about the room pacing, she reads...

"Jobs, like service workers, certain municipal workers, social workers, medical staff, fire fighters, police officers and other municipal employments will keep their positions... Non-necessity jobs will be shut down."

Oh dear god.

"That means me right!?" I jump from my seat on the couch waiting to be judged.

"I'll get to keep my job?"

"Yeah—It's, it's a..." Anita pulls up her phone to start reading again.

I pick up the conversation of my fate.

"Uh, yeah! I AM a service worker."

I CAN NOT BELIEVE THIS IS HAPPENING RIGHT NOW.

How could it come to this?! Sometimes I just wish I could join my brother in heaven.

I camp out in my cousin's bedroom to doom scroll.

Everyone on social media is prepping or complaining or talking about bible prophecy.

So many people are going to loose their jobs. It's all gonna be fine I'm sure but what is going to happen to the people? The economy, the housing market? I just can't believe it.

I am going to work? But if I am working, at what cost??? We'll have to what? How am I going to work? *With a plague mask on?*

THE PLAGUE.

I remember my time in history class going over the black plague. The classroom was small and cramped but roomy enough for the seats to be grouped into 6 desks. I sat with my high school friends.

The teacher, Mrs. Weirner, discussed how, during the Dark Ages and during the plague, plague doctors with bird-like masks and staffs with incense holders would go around inspecting patients for swollen armpits, a common symptom of the Black Plague.

Inside the masks, the plague doctors would hold an assortment of different types of herbs, like rosemary and thyme, and or spices they thought would keep away the bad "spirits" of the plague.

This has got to be the *worst* and maybe the longest spring break ever.

March, 17*th* 2020

I am still at my aunt's house, gnawing away at a leftover rib at 6:30pm, wondering if I can still make it this semester and how I am supposed to graduate this year. I fear I've fallen into a great big conundrum. I slump into the tan couch and grab the remote. A Chihuahua interrupts my existential crisis and curls up beside me, shivering. I turn on the news for proof of my fears.

The News reads...

BY MARCH 17th over 5,700 cases of the Corona virus are nation wide in the US and the death toll reached 105 people.

March 21*st* 2020

It's not over yet. My classes. All my hard work this year. NO. It can't be. Ive worked so hard for all of it I just. I can't believe that all of my classes are going to be online now. HOW AM I SUPPOSED TO GRASP ANY KNOWLEDGE?!?! I don't work that well with online classes, I need to be there in person. What if I have a question? or if I need instruction? I open up my emails to see if the professor answered. My After Effects Professor is terrible at answering my emails. He made a discord chat but, he made it so that he could decide who joins or not. In my mind, a voice rings in my head. 'How's that glass ceiling treating ya?' 'Not good not good at all.' I hang my head low, and sigh. 'Video games, have corrupted men's hearts, and minds.' 'Oh Lord, don't I know it.' 'Don't worry god will save you.' 'I hope.'

***

I go into work on March 31st 2020. Now, masks are mandatory— and gloves are recommended. My employer gave everyone an 'ESSENTIAL WORKER' red sign to place on the dash of our cars. I start my shift at at 8, wearing my provided blue mask and trying to breath.

Eventually, I get over-exhausted from bagging so many random strangers' groceries. My breath becomes so hot, it fogs up my glasses as I bag, so now I can't see. I try to wipe my glasses in between customers, but they just keep coming and my glasses just keep fogging up.

This could be the very definition of a personal hell...

I try to focus— heavy stuff first, then light, cold items go with cold and non-food items, always scan heavy items at the bottom of the cart— and place a sticker afterwards. I try to do all of this repeatedly with a debilitating mask on.

I am so secretly anxious, yet I've never felt so important.

One of the younger, dark-complexioned cashier women comes up to me.

"Wow, you are my hero..." she waves a little salute to me, grazing her rope braids.

"OH, me? Thanks, you're my hero too." I smile under my mask before throwing up a peace sign.

I receive a message from the discord chat:

Carmendlg: Are you off tomorrow?

Me: no

I work 12 to 6

Carmendlg: Hmmm

Gulag(Trent): is the campground even open

We were planning on going camping but with the way things are going we might as well camp out like homeless people somewhere in the local woods. It might give us some perspective.

Me: We can hang the night after tomorrow

Carmendlg: Ye it should be I don't see why not and Nah I work

Me: OOF

What about tonight?

Carmendlg: I am at work

LOL

I work overnight all week bc I needed the hours and the managers took over the day shifts.

Me: Welp

Carmendlg: F*** a quarantine.

***

March 23rd, 2020. Monday.

I come home after a 6 hour shift at 6pm.

"I am not feeling so good..." I am out of breath and my face feels raw from wearing a mask all day.

"It's like I am not breathing— I am not getting enough oxygen during work." I confide in my parents.

"Oh sweetie, I am starting to get worried for you Adriana."

"You are an essential worker..." My dad continues. "So you better take precautions—Masks aren't going to do anything!" My dad prattles on.

"She *NEEDS* her mask!"

"Cecilia, Cecilia, can I talk? Can I talk?" My dad lowers his open palm at her.

"—She needs to be at the hotel."

All I can hear them say is that I am a *liability,* that I am going to bring sickness to the family and they want me out of the house.

Dad goes to rest at his recliner again.

My mom exasperates and walks closer to me. "So is Carmen... She's a Service worker like you—she works at that hotel... Remember that hotel, honey?" She turns around to talk to dad on his recliner.

"Which one...?"

"The one!— the one from the side of the feeder road— you know!"

"The Homewood suites Hotel?"

"Yeah that one, the one your dad and I stayed at when we first moved to Kingwood." *I mean he does know.*

I can't believe my parents are actually trying to convince me to *stay, unsupervised, at a hotel with my best friend.*

Say less...

"You and Carmen are essential workers. You should talk to Carma."

I try not to think of it too much, ruminating in my mind as I lie motionless in my bed, overthinking about how I am going to get Covid-19.

How will I get Covid-19!

- From my lunch break

- Dirty toilet seat

- Someone throws a coughing fit at me

- Breathing to close to an infected person

- *I touch a grazing item* (Grazing: It's when an item that a customer has already started eating but they have us scan it after they eat it.)

I'm not sure if I am going about this the right way... There is no known cure for Covid-19 yet. So this has to be the way; *to protect my family*...

...I Have to live at a hotel...

***

March 24th 2020

I wake up to a text on my phone.

Carmen: Hey you wanna stay over at my hotel? My manager approved for us to stay at a full kitchen inlet room for about a month since we are both essential workers.

Me: really, are you sure your manager is okay with me staying???

Carmen: Yes, as long as we follow the rules and you sign in everyday and we share the same Hotel key.

Me: okay phew.

Carmen: Are you sure you sure you wanna go thru this?

Me: Yeah I mean this has to work.

Me: I mean yeah, I'll do it.

Carmen: To be honest, Adri, my mom has put me up to it, she asked my manager to lend us a room.

I put my phone down.

sigh.

16
Party

March 25th 2020

I enter the hotel room with my medium oversized, trusty carpet bag adorned with a painting of a Gondola drifting over the city of Venice.

"ohhhhhh I like your tote bag! Where did you get it?" Vanessa, Carmen's friend, is already there at the wooden table with a grocery bag of toiletries.

"Oh I got it from the Goodwill," I start to unpack my clothes into dressers.

"Ooooowhhhhh."

"How are you?" I ask her.

"I am good I just got a job at T-moblie."

"Oh, okay word." I nod.

"Yeah, I just really needed it.".... She stares down at the floor.

"Oh, I got everyone face masks!" Vanessa reaches for her bag.

I think she's talking about more medical grade masks.... I plop down on the couch again.

"Let's see—Oh skin care." But instead she pulls out a hand full of peel off masks.

We all burst out in laughter.

ahhh I sigh.

"This is nice, it's nice to ah— have a break especially since we are all essential workers risking our lives."

"—Kinda like we are all just waiting to get sick."

"Yeah," I lay back from the pillowed couch.

Vanessa organizes some groceries and plates and dishes for us in the humble blue kitchen inlet. Carmen and Vanessa chat about work and how life for each other was going, how Vanessa and our other friend Alana, the belly dancer, had to leave her job at Sally's, the beautician retail store (a non-essential job).

I am really starting to worry about Alana's safety.

"Doesn't this couch also turn into a bed?"

"Yeah it does."

I spend the next couple of days going to the dollar tree and good wills to find cheap, inexpensive dinnerware and rags and pot holders to suffice our needs since a lot of fast food places shut down.

I want to live and let be, but something in me wants to be free, to be free to travel and explore the world and yet here I am scurrying in a dollar tree for a hand made rug. Where does all this stuff come from anyway? I hope it's all recycled plastics. This stay-cation could be really awesome...

The next day...

"This could be a good learning experience for you." My mom starts, as I am packing away my sewing kit, paint supplies, knitting, sketchbook, colored pencils – anything that could satisfy my hobbies and interests. Staying busy like this is better than wasting time on video games.

"Yeah, mom I know." I drop a colored pencil from my dangling book bag.

"You need to get out more. I am serious, Adri." She continues. "There comes a time when everyone has to leave the nest."

"Yeah like a baby bird, a bird that is already there, but the wings are not strong enough. And then you fly, and then ahhhh." She holds out her hands like two birds and make them fly, "and then fall."

I look down.

She continues, "Not fall but just. Like 'I can do it' 'I can do it.'" Her hands fly up and teeter.

I rub my eyes.

"I just want you to be able to sustain yourself." She rests her hands.

"I want it to all come true for you... But you live..." She gestures to my light blue ocean themed room.

"Not like this..."

"Here." She goes downstairs and hands me a pack of q-tips to clean my ears.

Thursday March 26,2020

I grab an apple from the fruit bowl that Carmen left out for us. And take a bite.

"So wanna go to the gym?"

"Yeah, we could go for a while."

The hotel has a small but a gym we have access to. We work out at night, no one's there anyway.

"Hey, how did you get to be so tall?" Carmen asks me.

"What?" I ask as I am walking on the elliptical. Just getting in those steps, trying to feel as normal as possible by exercising, I get restless legs and need to jog before I go into a depressive spiral.

"I am 220, and I am 5.2."

"Oh wow, that's about my weight but I am 5.5."

She puts in her headphones and starts working out.

I don't blame her; she has more weight than me, but she's still so beautiful. She's been through so much... And when you go through stress, the body holds onto weight like a lonely, scared child holding onto a doll. I feel her pain.

Friday, March 27 2020

I am sitting on the Hotel couch with Carmen, sewing up a new mask made of this scrappy material. We watch Akira from the Fire Stick attachment I plugged into the back of the TV.

"It's getting late..." She says mid-way through the movie.

"Oh," I look up from my DIY mask that ends up tattering and falling. I probably reek from today's work day.

"Imma take a shower." I say under my breath. She nodds.

"Yeah."

"Yeah." I pack up my sewing bag.

"We should watch the movie Contagion next!" I smile my mischievous smile.

"NO, No no," she says with a tinge of fear in her voice.

"Come on, the disease in contagion is much worse than Covid."

"Just don't wanna!" *'Ouch'* It's always the bats. Okay, she gets up and moves to get her clothes from the laundry.

We agreed that she would do laundry and I would do dishes, since she knows exactly where everything is in the Hotel, including all the laundry machines and ice machines.

Saturday March 26th 2020

I come back from a grueling day at work to find a pile of trash from all the food I bought and a pile of dishes stacked up. It looked like someone's play kitchen toys are all stacked high.

I honestly was so happy to be free from constant nagging from my parents. Like I could finally live and let live. I spent a day off from work doing dishes and enjoying it. I imagined being in southern France, whistling a tune while wearing a flowered print cloth dress with a black apron.

We watched the news in waves: in the morning testimonies, people finding work from home, government handouts, talks of stimulus checks, ... banning Tumblr porn...

Sunday March 27th 2020

"Oh! Hey." Carmen walks in at 6am to me painting a 12 x 6 painting of an angel on the wooden hotel table.

"Hey, hey I couldn't sleep last night."

My eyes are glued to my painting and my hand is as steady as a moth on a wire.

She steps back to look at it.

"It's wow."

"Yeah."

Monday 28, 2020

I work a double shift.

Tuesday 29th 2020

Me and Carmen are chilling one day, watching Tiger king on Netflix on her laptop on the table and eating popcorn popped over the stove top.

"Hey, I am bringing a few friends over for a few drinks."

"OH, are you sure that's okay?" I ask while putting away some hand towels. "Yeah Trent's coming, my friend Marcia, Jada, I don't know if Meg can make it."

I go outside to look at the moon for a bit before coming back inside.

I come back to the table and I get the music going, with some smashing pumpkins. And I put a bottle of Vodka out on the table.

"So"...

"Did you watch the movie Serendipity?"

"Yeah I did."

Everyone starts giggling.

"Anddddd???"

"Enough!" Okay I can feel my cheeks start to turn red.

"She's not like us."

"Please tell me the story of when you were little."

"Which one?"

"The one about when you dared your best friend to eat a raw piece of garlic."

"Oohhhh man...." We pass around the bottle in a circle.

I sit criss cross in a circle to meditate.

The group just starts talking about whatever...

I am calm.

I breathe. And count. . . And exhale. . .

Carmen starts to join me.

Trent looks at us, "Ugh, Hippies man." And swigs down the rest of the bottle.

Easter Celebration:

April 2nd, 2020

I leave work early and it turns out they don't need me to work because of the 6-foot rule they implemented, as there won't be long line of people waiting for their basic essential needs.

I break away and become a part of the customer line to buy ingredients for cake balls as a part of an easter celebration. Well, I haven't celebrated Easter, not since I was 11.

My parents are very devout, I mean non-denominational.

We don't celebrate easter.

We don't celebrate St. Patrick's day.

We don't celebrate Halloween.

We just don't celebrate holidays.

Like secular people do.

It's nice to have this moment to be by myself, and sometimes with my best friend in this humble hotel.

I arrive at the hotel with a pep in my step and groceries in my hand.

I 'accidentally' took a bag of spaghetti

(but I was desperate)

… better than being a kidnapper… Tch.

I unloaded my groceries into the hotel cabinets.

"Okay, let's see what we got here."

"Cake mix check, pre-made frosting, sprinkles."

Spaghetti.

I try boiling it in the pot but it burned terribly . . .

Krap. . . 'Ugh, I can't catch a break, can I?'

'Not even a break to pee. . .'